4.2

COLLECTING, ARRANGING, PRESSING
AND DRYING FLOWERS

FLOWER
Art

EDITED BY MIKE DARTON

COLLECTING, ARRANGING, PRESSING
AND DRYING FLOWERS

FLOWER
Art

EDITED BY MIKE DARTON

TIGER BOOKS INTERNATIONAL
LONDON

A QUINTET BOOK

This edition first published 1989 by
Tiger Books International Ltd.
London

Copyright © 1989 Quintet Publishing Limited
ISBN 1 85501 034 8

This book was designed and produced by
Quintet Publishing Limited
6 Blundell Street
London N7 9BH

Creative Director: Peter Bridgewater
Art Director: Ian Hunt
Designer: Annie Moss
Project Editor: Mike Darton
Editor: Belinda Giles

Typeset in Great Britain by
Central Southern Typesetters, Eastbourne
Manufactured in Hong Kong by
Regent Publishing Services Limited
Printed in Hong Kong by
Leefung–Asco Printers Limited

The material in this publication previously
appeared in *The Painted Garden, The Classic
Horticulturist, Flower Works, Flower Arranging,
Step-by-Step Flower Arranging* and *Pressed
Flowercraft.*

Contents

Introduction

There are many books on flower arranging. There are almost as many on the history of collecting and growing flowers for botanical science or just for pleasure. There are a number of books too on different things to do with flowers, such as creating pots pourris, or making artificial flowers. There are a few books on pressing flowers and making presentations of them. And there are even fewer books on drying flowers and making presentations of them. This book successfully combines all these themes in one colourful compilation.

Above all, this book is intended to be practical – to give information on what can be done, and how to do it, with flowers. Even the historical section is centred on the notion that after perusing it the reader may wish to do his or her own bit of exploring for unusual species – even today new species are being discovered at a surprising rate – or at least to pursue the interest through additional reading and research.

Flower arranging is a strange mixture of expertise, artistry and experience – strange, because although artistry (or an eye for design) is only one of those three contributory elements, each resulting arrangement is judged almost solely in terms of the viewer's subjective idea of artistic merit. And people have very different ideas about what is visually appealing. A successful arrangement that is considered attractive by a large majority of the people who see it, then, may owe far more to expertise and experience than many of those same viewers ever realize. That expertise and experience can be passed on, and in this book – together with the basic principles of design – an attempt is made to do just that. In particular, there is an extensive illustrated list of flowers that are most useful for arranging, presented in the order of the seasons in which each becomes available.

Later in the book there are two further sections on special flower arrangements – making up a presentation bouquet, making table decorations, preparing floral accoutrements for weddings and christenings, and so forth – both similarly well illustrated.

Flower pressing is rewarding for many reasons, one of them being its potential for variety and change. Again presentation represents a combination of expertise, artistry and experience, and again expertise and experience tend to be undervalued contributory factors – although, as with flower arranging, someone who actually does have an unusually good sense of design may come up with excellent

RIGHT Banksia serrata, *the red honeysuckle or saw Banksia, is an especially gnarled plant with red flower spikes that turn into woody cones as the seeds set.*

results straight away. If the right flowers are picked in the right condition – and once more a beautifully illustrated list of useful flowers and plants, each listed by its season of availability, is included in the book – and pressed according to the principles outlined here, attractive designs and combinations should be virtually assured. A few years ago presentation was limited largely to the creation of pictures. Now, however, suppliers are selling an increasingly wide range of settings and background materials, and there are enormous possibilities for the production of decorated pendants, pill-boxes and trinket boxes, plaques and paper-weights, cards and bookmarks. Some truly exquisite work is within the reach of anyone with a modicum of patience and persistence.

Drying flowers is at present a rather uncommon pastime. The technique is fully described in this book, however, together with some picturesque arrangements of the dried products.

Also included is a brief section on the 'language of flowers' – what specific flowers are popularly held to express when presented as a gift – proof of the emotive qualities attributed to flowers from Victorian times.

ABOVE The Art Deco-style figurine was the inspiration for this arrangement. She is rather pretty, and makes a nice addition to a floral grouping.
Materials: tin can with soaked floral foam, blue base, figurine. Bride gladioli, delphiniums, Singapore orchids.

Collecting :
A SHORT HISTORY

Horticulture was being practised long before the Hanging Gardens of Babylon were built in about 600BC. The Assyrians collected plants for their temple gardens and there are detailed records of ancient Egyptians growing figs, pomegranates and grapes. The lush silts of the Nile valley, refertilized every year by the river's winter floods, must have provided rich harvests. Queen Hatshepsut was introducing incense trees into her new temple garden between 1500 and 1485BC, and, during the reign of Rameses III (1198–1167BC), trees and shrubs were grown in decorated containers. Egyptian gardens had a line and formality that undoubtedly influenced the Romans, and were in due course to be adopted by the

BELOW A painting from the Egyptian tomb of Nebamon, dating from c.1400BC. Here we see not only fruit trees in cultivation but also the use of water.

ABOVE A small herb garden could accommodate a dozen useful culinary herbs – parsley, dill, mint, sage, rhyme, rosemary, garlic, chives, coriander, hyssop, winter savory and chamomile – in a neat arrangement of stone slabs and beds.

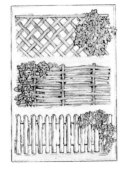

ABOVE *Trellis, wattle and picket fences can all be used to enclose a garden, or part of it, and provide excellent support for climbers like roses or clematis.*

Italians. Today, most good gardens have a great deal in common with those found at the source of Western civilization several thousand years ago.

On the other side of the world the Chinese, during the Ch'in and Han dynasties, were developing the art of landscaping. Their approach seems to have been naturalistic – they enhanced natural scenery with artificial mountains, rock gardens and pools. No doubt shrubs such as the Buddleia were enjoyed both in gardens and in the wild. The idea was to create an area for quiet meditation.

The Chinese were probably the first to use flowers to any great degree in cooking as they have many varied floral recipes from as long ago as 3000 BC. Not only were flowers used to add flavour and colour, but eating them was considered to be beneficial to the body.

Further west, the Greeks were the leaders in establishing a culinary flower culture, followed by the Romans, with whom rose petals were a particular favourite. The petals were extensively used to scent and decorate dishes and drinks, especially at banquets and festivals for, as the Chinese ate chrysanthemums so the Romans ate rose petals – albeit, for a somewhat different reason – as they were believed to prevent, or even cure, drunkenness. Rose water

BELOW *The Roman garden: a trompe l'oeil* fresco *in the Empress Livia's villa by the Prima Porte, Rome.*

was first mentioned in 140 BC in the writings of the Roman poet and doctor Nicander.

Dioscorides (fl. 1st century) was a Greek, practising herbal medicine at about the time that *The Acts of the Apostles* was being written. He wrote a book about pharmacology, *De Materia Medica,* that was to be used for the next 1500 years. He described the medicinal properties of 600 plants, and had the goodness to provide all the known names (around the Middle East at any rate) for each plant. He lists 13 for *Cylamen hederifolium* – a good example of why a single, internationally recognized name for each plant is such a necessity today.

Information about Roman gardens can be found in the works of Pliny the Elder (AD23–79). In spite of a heavy workload, he managed to write a phenomenal number of books. His *Natural History* runs to 37 'volumes' in one of which he describes how a *topiarius* (not exactly someone to do the topiary, but a man employed to train creepers over statues and to keep growth in the gardens tidy) could dwarf planes and conifers with a technique similar to *Bonsai.*

Pliny the Younger (Gaius Plinius Caecilius Secundus) had a lot to say about the plants and gardens of his day. Clearly, Roman gardening had much in common with the modern art, and many Roman plants are enjoyed to this day.

We know little about what kind of horticulture was being practised in Europe between the decline of the Roman Empire and the Renaissance because records are scarce. We do know, however, that after William the Conqueror's invasion of Britain in 1066, the development of new monasteries helped to preserve some of the species the Romans left behind.

From the Middle Ages to Tudor Times

The Norman monks must certainly have brought their skills to England: they have been credited with introducing pinks, wallflowers and other plants grown for medicine.

The 12th century writer Alexander Neckham (1157–1217) describes such monastic gardening in his *De Naturis Rerum,* although whether he gleaned from practical observation or lifted from earlier literature is not clear.

Also during the Middle Ages the Knights of the Cross of St John, returning from the Crusades, brought recipes using flowers and flower waters to England to add to those based on indigenous flowers.

We can tell from paintings like the Wilton Diptych (c.1395) that certain garden flowers were in cultivation. There are double roses, violets and irises at the Virgin Mary's feet. European wildflowers – sea catchfly and liverwort *(Silene*

vulgaris and *Hepatica)* – are also shown, and were certainly being grown in the monastery gardens. Although their primary use was probably medicinal, their decorative properties must have been appreciated for them to have been used in such an artistic context.

By the 15th century, horticulture was making progress again. Between 1400 and 1440, the aptly named Mayster Ion Gardener wrote a treatise called *The Feate of Gardening.* Ion Gardener's text is highly practical and concerns itself solely with the culture of plants for utility. Novel techniques like the grafting of pear trees on to hawthorn are covered.

Of the 97 plants described in *The Feate of Gardening,* 26 had been introduced from outside Britain. No doubt there were other exotics being grown in monastery gardens and in the green households, but the large-scale collecting of plants had yet to begin.

However, with the Tudors, innovation became widespread. Sir Thomas More wrote *Utopia* (1516), in which gardens figure as places with attractive flowers and well tended fruit (More had fine gardens laid out for himself at Chelsea).

The Elizabethan Era

In Italy, at this time the epicentre of the Renaissance, gardening was progressing at a greater pace than anywhere else in Christendom. One result of the reborn interest in science was the birth of the botanic garden, the idea springing from the renewed interest in ancient literature: the first botanic gardens in the world were in Pisa and Padua. Elsewhere, plant collecting was to become fashionable, particularly among royalty.

It was into this period of growing interest in new plants that Jules Charles L'Ecluse (Clusius) was born. Clusius was a great botanist and plant collector. With his sound technical education, he was able to observe and record botanical details with unprecedented accuracy.

From 1565, he spent a year or so plant hunting in Spain and Portugal. This was interesting for him not just because he could study the native plants but also because the Spanish and Portuguese were at the time bringing exotic plants home from the New World. It is possible that potatoes were already being grown in Spain as early as 1565, a couple of decades before Raleigh grew them in England, and Clusius may have observed them there – although he does not refer to them until much later, when he recalls in his *Rariorum Plantarum Historia* (1601) that he had the plant in 1588.

On his visit to Britain (1571) he read Spanish physician Nicholas Monardes' book about American plants, and trans-

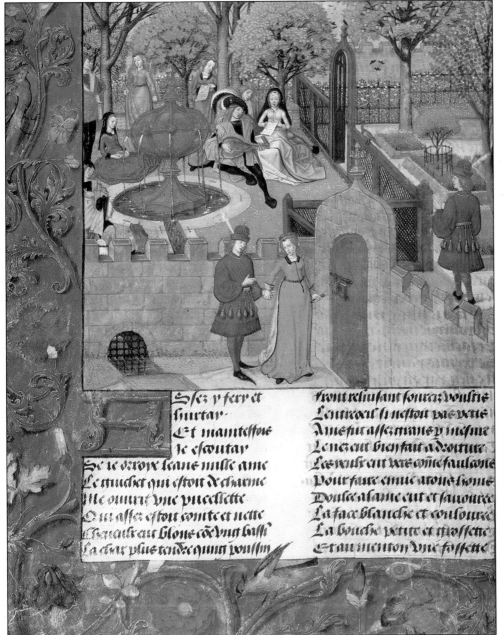

LEFT *Garden scene from the medieval manuscript of* Le Romaunt de la Rose, *c.1485, showing the courtly lover first seeking admission to, and then walking within, the enclosed garden.*

lated it into Latin (the *lingua franca* of the 16th-century scholars) for use in Europe. (Frampton's English translation was not published until 1596.)

In Elizabeth I's reign the knot garden developed. This consisted of a small area of convoluted hedgery with paths or beds in between. Hedging material was usually box or rosemary, and the beds were filled with coloured gravels or with flowering plants. Knot gardens were not very large – certainly not as large as the impressive French-style parterres.

Small gardens, although they probably contained some plants for beauty, were mainly functional.

A prominent member of the Barber-Surgeons' Company was one John Gerard. Over the years, Gerard has come in for more than his fair share of lambast. Criticism of his *Herball* is well justified on many counts, but it does contain some original work and is an important example of Elizabethan botanical literature. His personality and humour radiate from the text.

Collecting in the 1600s

The lives of the two John Tradescants, father and son, ran from the glorious days of Queen Elizabeth through to the first couple of years of the Interregnum under Oliver Cromwell. John Tradescant the Elder was the son of a Suffolk yeoman who had moved to London. His first recorded job was with Lord Salisbury, whose gardens were in London and at Hatfield House, some miles north. Hatfield was being revamped, and Tradescant was sent to find new trees for the avenues, fruits and vegetables for the orchards, and flowers for the 'pleasure gardens'. He introduced new grapevines, white mulberry – in the hope of starting silk production in England – and a number of new roses from France. By 1614 he had left Hatfield and moved to Kent, where he worked as gardener to Sir Edward Wotton.

A few years later, sponsored by Salisbury, he joined Sir Dudley Digges on what turned out to be a most fruitful expedition to Russia. Among many new introductions he brought back seeds of the first larch trees to be grown in Britain.

An obsessive nature, acute powers of observation and an indefatigable spirit – as with so many great horticulturalists – spurred Tradescant Senior to greater achievements than those of any ordinary gardener. Descriptions of his travels, some of which are on record in his diaries, throw considerable light on his character.

By the time John Tradescant the Elder had accepted the job of running the Duke of Buckingham's garden, his talented son, John Tradescant the Younger, was ready to leave King's School, Canterbury, and start an equally successful career in horticulture.

The most important events of his career were his three trips to North America between 1637 and 1654. He was responsible for providing us with so many species which today are commonplace that it is hard for us to imagine what life was like without them.

RIGHT Spring, *a painting by Abel Grimmer in the 16th century, thought to be copied from a Brueghel original. It illustrates the development of raised beds for herbs and flowers.*

ABOVE The frontispiece from Gerard's Herball, *as originally printed in 1597.*

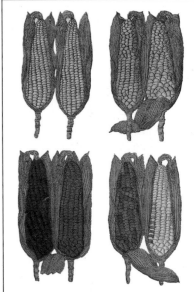

ABOVE *Maize (Indian corn), as illustrated in Gerard's* Herball.

By the time Charles II came to the throne, the style was changing. Although French influence was to dominate garden design for some time to come, the growing interest in plants for their own sake was beginning to necessitate a change in the principles. It is impossible to grow a miscellany of interesting plants in a parterre without ruining it, so it became necessary to provide areas where the special needs of the new style of gardening could be catered for.

John Evelyn (1620–1706) was the first writer to describe a heated greenhouse (at the Apothecaries' Garden, Chelsea). In a later publication he describes a design of his own. Many now know him for his diaries, which describe his milieu, although not half so well as do those of Samuel Pepys. But he was a keen and educated gardener with a particular knowledge of trees. His book *Sylva, or A Discourse of Forest Trees* (1664) was a standard work to be used for another 100 years. Evelyn's own garden at Sayes Court in Deptford, London, was well known, and he frequently describes it in his diary.

Towards the end of the 17th century, the increasing demand for plants presented commercial nurserymen with novel opportunities. The passion for standing hundreds of elegant pots about the place, each one planted with decorative 'greens', was at its height. The number of species and varieties in cultivation grew bigger every year but, until this time, most nursery stock was imported, mainly from Holland. By 1700, George London had started the first large professional nursery of its kind in England.

The Eighteenth Century

While the fashion for 'greens' was fading, the urge to collect plant species was still as strong as ever. Botanic and physic gardens existed all over Europe, and new introductions were continuing to pour into cultivation. Breeding, too, was fast developing.

In 1722 Sir Hans Sloane, himself a keen botanist, purchased a parcel of riverside ground from Charles Cheyne, very close to where Sir Thomas More's estate had been in Henry VIII's reign, and conveyed it to the Apothecaries' Company, subject to certain conditions: the garden was to be properly managed and, for 40 years, 50 new species per year were to be grown in the garden. A dried, mounted specimen of each new plant was to be presented to the Royal Society. This ensured that at least 2,000 new plants would be introduced before 1762. The apothecaries appointed a professional florist as gardener, and in Philip Miller they made a wise choice. He was to work at the Physic Garden for a staggering 48 years.

His *Gardeners' and Florists' Dictionary* (1724) became the standard reference work for florists for more than a century. His encyclopaedic knowledge of plants and his practical background were helpful, but in addition to these qualities, he was lucky enough to be possessed of green fingers.

ABOVE Linnaeus in the costume of a Laplander. His tour of Lapland in 1732 led to a detailed study of the flora.

ABOVE The Gardens in the Parc Mirabell, Austria, painted by N. Diesel in around 1720, illustrates a French-style parterre de broderie, a pattern of garden developed from the earlier knot gardens.

ABOVE RIGHT The Chinese Kiosk at Woodside House, Berkshire, portrayed by Thomas Robins in around 1755, showing some of the gardeners at work.

Miller received Linnaeus at Chelsea in 1736, and the fact that the great man visited at all, shows how much the garden, with its extensive collection of rare plants, had grown in international stature since Miller's appointment.

Miller, in his declining years, made the mistake of clinging too long to his appointment. The fame of the Chelsea garden became overshadowed by Kew which, under the vigorous management of William Aiton, became the botanist's Mecca. However, to this day the Chelsea Physic Garden remains an important repository of rare plants.

During the eighteenth century the culinary use of flowers became even more prolific. Nearly every type of flower was tried in some way or another, often with no knowledge of the hazards hidden within the pretty blooms. Rose petals were also used in sandwiches as a summertime treat and were made into a conserve, a fragrant, syrupy jam, for spreading on scones and teacakes in the winter.

Towards the end of the 18th century, French influence declined. English love of nature was breaking through the strictures of regimented planting. Parterres were going; broad, sweeping lawns were coming in. By 1760, work at Stourhead had begun, and with it came the fashion of constructing lakes large enough to reflect a topography decorated with trees and shrubs. The second half of the century saw the works of the great landscapers Lancelot 'Capability' Brown and Humphry Repton.

When the English botanist Sir Joseph Banks sailed from Plymouth aboard the *Endeavour* in 1768 as a paying member on James Cook's first great voyage of discovery into the Pacific he took along his naturalist friend Dr Daniel Solander, Linnaeus's favourite pupil, as his right-hand man.

Cook circumnavigated the world, visiting Tahiti, Brazil, Australia, New Zealand, the East Indies and South Africa, while Banks crammed the small ship with drawings and dried specimens of some 3,000 plant species, of which 1,000 were completely new to science. The engravings from this voyage have been preserved as Banks' *Florilegium*.

The voyage caused a sensation and made Banks' reputation as a pivotal figure in the scientific establishment. His London house in Soho Square, with its natural history collections and a magnificent library run by Solander, became a mecca for visiting scientists.

His reign at the Royal Society paralleled the rule of Kew as the major botanic institution in England, sending out dozens of intrepid plant hunters, many recommended by Banks. These peripatetic botanists included such luminaries as Francis Masson, Allan Cunningham, David Nelson, George Caley, William Ker, Peter Good and James Bowie, all of whom made invaluable contributions to botany.

The era of Banks' tutelage over the botanic establishment ended with his death in 1820, when Kew was superseded by the Royal Horticultural Society.

Gardens and Collectors of the 1800s

By 1800 the English style of garden, as typified by places like Stourhead, was beginning to influence the world as strongly as had the French 100 years before. Areas colonized by the British were to inherit their style of gardening. Climate made a difference to the type of plants used, but not to the style. One of the finest examples in the tropics is at Peradeniya, Sri Lanka, started in 1821. Botanic gardens were laid out also in Singapore (1822), Trinidad (1819) and Jamaica (1774). One of the loveliest, not only for its layout with lawns, natural groups of trees and flowering plants, but also for its magnificent position in a quiet harbour cove, is at Sydney, Australia.

Small gardens, too, were beginning to develop. Changes in the social structure of the civilized world were to mean changes in gardening habits. One of the first visionaries to herald this new age was John Claudius Loudon. Loudon was born in 1783 near Edinburgh, where he went to school until he was 14. His thirst for knowledge of all kinds was prodigious. Because of his love of plants, his father sent him as an apprentice to a local nurseryman, under whom he studied trees and their culture with such intensity that he soon became an authority.

As an excessively hard worker, it is not surprising that Loudon had managed to make himself pretty well off by the time he was 30. His *Encyclopaedia of Gardening,* published in 1822, was aimed at people who, like himself, were fairly new to gracious living. The *Encyclopaedia* is a 'how to' book of roughly 1.1 million words with helpful illustrations and descriptions. First comes a long section about the history of gardening, followed by details of tooling-up for the estate, man-management and plants. It has been compared with Mrs Beeton's *Household Management,* doing for small estate management what she did for housekeeping.

In 1826 he launched one of the first popular gardening magazines: *The Gardeners' Magazine.*

After he had undergone a serious surgical operation, his wife Jane helped him to complete his most important book, *Arboretum et Fruticetum Britannicum,* a massive undertaking in eight volumes, published in 1838. She was also producing her own *Gardening for Ladies* (1840) and the *Ladies' Companion* series at this time.

The Loudons' love of naturalism in landscapes and gardens, although it went out of fashion for a generation, set the trend for modern 'informal' gardening. Although one can still find uncomfortable reminders of the Victorian bedding craze in public parks, corporation traffic islands and certain private gardens, much of today's popular garden-

RIGHT Kitchen Garden at Plankenberg, *a painting of a somewhat untidy country vegetable plot by J. E. Schindler in 1885. Red and green cabbages, turnips, beans and sunflowers are being grown.*

ABOVE An illustration from Jane Loudon's Ladies' Flower Garden of Ornamental Perennials *(1844).*

ABOVE *An individual plan for a small parterre.*

ing stems from Loudon's original philosophy, improved and interpreted by the great gardeners of the last 100 years.

In the 1880s, the strong backlash against hard, formal planting was led by a gardener called William Robinson. Born in Ireland in 1838, Robinson worked in a number of Irish gardens before crossing the sea in 1861 to take up work in Regents Park, London. By this time, the mania for carpet bedding was at its height in England. Encouraged by trendsetters like Joseph Paxton, ostentation and artificially ruled. Gardens were laid out in great wedges of lurid colours, punctuated by bushes clipped into peculiar shapes and surrounded by banks of depressing evergreens. Obelisks, urns and curiosities abounded.

At Regents Park he was put in charge of the herbaceous section, and was promoted rapidly. He began to collect wild flowers and, on country excursions, became familiar with the English cottages. He delighted in the jumble of plants in their gardens – herbs, fruit and flowers all apparently planted without any special design and yet all with specific uses. His observations inspired him to begin a career of garden writing.

Robinson began several magazines. In 1872, after a trip to North America, he launched *The Garden,* which was financially disappointing but enabled him to further his crusade. *Gardening Illustrated* began in 1879 and was to run until 1956, when it merged with *Gardener's Chronicle*. Several

ABOVE *The formal layout of the gardens at* Wilton House, *depicted by E. Adveno Brooke in around 1857. Today, much of the carpet-bedded planting has been replaced by grass and trees.*

ABOVE *Layout for a small potager with vegetables separated by narrow brick paths, enclosed by a low clipped box hedge.*

other periodicals were produced during his life. In 1883 his most important work, *The English Flower Garden,* was published.

Robinson was a lover of wild flowers and of trees. In his lifetime he was to plant hundreds of thousands of them. He was also to set the trend towards naturalistic planting.

Robinson's penchant for naturalism was also evident in Australia, championed by William Robert Guilfoyle, the man who created Melbourne's superb Botanic Gardens in their present form.

Guilfoyle wrought radical changes. Inspired by such 18th century masters of the 'natural' style as Lancelot 'Capability' Brown, he altered the entire landscape, uprooting and re-positioning trees to open up broad vistas so that the gardens resembled the grounds of an English estate. Throughout the grounds clumps of flowering shrubs, rhododendrons, azaleas and camellias added colour and broke up the landscape. It was a carefully contrived marriage of nature and artifice.

LEFT A simple knot of clipped box, with cypresses at the corners and a formally planted bed, with an ornamental standard, in the centre.

RIGHT The Nicolsons created the gardens at Sissinghurst from a ruin. This is the so-called cottage garden in the grounds.

From the Turn of the Century

Robinson may have started the trend toward naturalistic gardening but Gertrude Jekyll perfected the style. Robinson and Jekyll were friends for many years and worked together on *The Garden,* which she edited when he stood down.

It is fashionable today to rank Jekyll as one of the greatest figures in the history of horticulture. That she has had a profound influence on modern gardening is indisputable. Her colour schemes, her plant associations, her treatment of wild gardens and her approach to garden layout can be seen everywhere.

Jekyll's genius lay in her ability to place the right plants together. She was able to combine their different characteristics – not only their colours – to create an artistic whole, much as any artist makes use of the materials at his or her disposal. To do this successfully is more difficult than it sounds, and even in the best gardens there are near misses.

Vita Sackville-West, although she met Jekyll only once, was probably deeply influenced by her. Her garden at Sissinghurst certainly bears all the Jekyll trademarks. Her triumph is the rose garden, where she fostered many varieties of old rose that had gone so far out of fashion they were in danger of extinction. She and her husband Harold Nicolson rescued one unfamiliar rose which was growing in the rubbish when they moved in; it was thought by some to be 'Rose de Maures', previously considered extinct, and was reintroduced as 'Sissinghurst Castle'.

By 1961 Sissinghurst was open to the public regularly, and was a delight to stroll through at any time of the year. Vita Sackville-West, then nearly 70, was forced to give up her writing because of illness. She died of cancer in 1962.

There were many important collectors at the beginning of the 20th century – men like E. H. Wilson, Reginald Farrer, William Purdom and Frank Kingdon-Ward – but one who was not only a collector but a fine gardener as well was E. A. Bowles.

Edward Augustus Bowles was born, lived and died in the same house. He was never short of money and never had to earn a living. Many in his position would have contributed little to society but, not counting his extensive work for charity, Bowles provided horticulture with a superb legacy of plants. His garden writing is steeped with expertise but at the same time entertains. His rugged support of the Royal Horticultural Society over half a century has been too valuable to calculate.

Bowles' strength was in his ability to identify a plant quickly and accurately. Although, like Gertrude Jekyll, his eyesight was by no means perfect, he had acute powers of observation. As a talented artist he was able to illustrate his own books on crocuses, *Colchicum,* and daffodils. His drawings are not only botanically accurate, they are a delight to look at. His main contribution to garden literature was the trilogy *My Garden in Spring* (1914), *My Garden in Summer* (1914) and *My Garden in Autumn and Winter* (1915).

Arranging

EQUIPMENT

A selection of the correct tools and equipment can help tremendously in flower arranging to build up confidence and prevent frustration. If you start your collection with one or two basic pieces and add others as and when they are needed, or as your skills progress, the initial cost will not be too great. Choose well-designed equipment which should be easy and comfortable to use.

You will need a good heavy pinholder, a pair of flower scissors or pruners, about 1½ft (45cm) of 2–2½in (5–6.3cm) wire mesh, a block of water-retaining floral foam and a small amount of adhesive clay for anchoring arrangements (available in rolls as Oasis-Fix). Florists and garden centres sell foam and pinholders, and wire mesh can be bought at hardware shops.

PINHOLDERS are available in several sizes. They are useful for anchoring Japanese-style designs and also for securing heavy branches.

SCISSORS There are several very good makes now available in varying price ranges. If possible, try one or two for 'grip' and test the weight and balance in your hand.

FLORAL FOAM is available in several makes but you should experiment with the various options to find out which one suits your particular needs. There are two distinct types; the green one used for fresh arrangements and the pale brown, dry one used exclusively for dried and fabric flower designs. The brown foam is much more dense and solid and should never be soaked. Conversely, the green variety is not solid enough to hold stems firmly and should not be used dry.

Each type is available in several shapes and sizes.

OASIS-FIX is a dark green, malleable substance similar in texture to Plasticine, a modelling clay. It has a toffee-like appearance which never sets completely hard, but will stick almost any dry surfaces together. It is used extensively for attaching wired flowers to their bases, for securing a receptacle inside another container, and also for fixing candle-cups to vases or candlesticks. It does not, however, adhere safely to glass or highly-glazed surfaces.

PRONGS are made from pale green plastic and have four long pins on to which a block of foam is impaled for greater stability.

A SHARP KNIFE is an indispensable piece of equipment. It can be used for trimming all kinds of stems, and for pointing the tips so that they can be driven easily into foam. It can also be used for cutting floral foam and for removing thorns from rose stems.

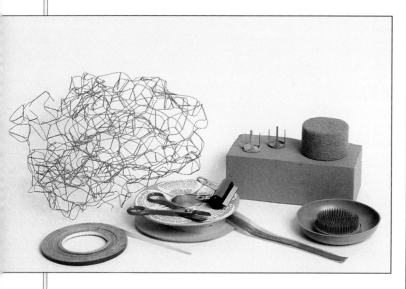

ABOVE Minimum equipment: *(left to right) 1 Floral tape. 2 Wire mesh. 3 Mini-secateurs. 4 Bulldog clip. 5 Oasis-fix. 6 Oasis pin. 7 Large block of green foam. 8 Dry foam for dried and fabric arrangements. 9 Small oasis bowl.*

ABOVE Full basic equiment: *1 Well-designed watering can. 2 Packets of long-life powder for fresh flowers. 3 Oasis-fix, an oil-based fixative which can be removed from surfaces with white spirit. 4 Narrow-bladed knife sufficiently long to cut through soaked foam. 5 and 6 Stainless steel scissors and mini-secateurs, which are light, well-balanced and easy to handle. 7 Clear adhesive tape about ⅜in (10mm) wide. 8 White vase. 9 Dry foam used for dried and fabric flower arrangements. 10 Large block of green foam – easily cut when soaked in water or a long-life solution. 11 Small cylindrical shape of green foam – a convenient size for plastic saucers and small containers. 12 Plastic water spray and mister. 13 Small plastic saucer. 14 Prongs.*

SHEARS with long-blades such as those used in the kitchen and by dressmakers, are also very handy for flower arrangers. They are ideal for cutting ribbon, fabric and fine wire. For the very heavy wire stems of some fabric flowers and foliage, you will need small secateurs, and for large woody branches, you will need gardening secateurs.

CLEAR ADHESIVE TAPE may be used for securing the foam to the container, especially for heavy designs, or if the arrangement has to be moved. Smaller designs will be sufficiently firm if the foam is simply impaled on a prong.

CLEARLIFE is a colourless spray which helps to prolong the vase life of some fresh flowers. It prevents them from shattering, and flowers such as larkspur, delphinium, cornflower and eremurus, indeed, any that drop their petals, can be held a little longer with a light spray when the arrangement is completed.

A **WATERING CAN** is quite indispensable for watering house plants and also for adding water to flower arrangements when necessary. Even though you may previously have thoroughly soaked the foam and added water initially, there is bound to be some dehydration.

A **SPRAY** is very handy for giving your arrangements a final spray with clear water – obviously when you have spent time and trouble making the design you want it to last as long as possible. In addition to providing water for the stems a daily spray with a mister helps to keep the materials really fresh, especially if the room is warm during hot weather.

RIBBONS can be an elegant addition to many flower arrangements and gifts so the more colours you have to choose from, the better. The polypropylene or paper ribbon in particular is excellent for decorating bouquets. Woven ribbon, as opposed to the paper variety, is available in a wide range of colours and widths and is relatively water-tolerant.

CANDLE-CUPS are available in gold, black or white. They are small containers specially shaped with a 'foot' that can be fitted into the neck of a bottle or candlestick.

COLOUR SPRAYS may be needed now and again to complement a special colour scheme, such as gold, silver and bronze around Christmas-time. Old containers can be quickly revitalized with spray paint and new ones can be 'antiquated' using a combination of sprays.

Proprietary brand sprays can also be applied to living flowers and foliage, wood, plastic and even candles – to change or enhance their original colours. The sprays, however, should be used on living material with very great care and treated as an expedient rather than a general practice.

STUB WIRES are useful for supporting flowers whose stems might become curved as they take up water. Note: a wire support should never be used to revitalize a fading flower but rather to control a fresh one. If support is necessary, try to insert the wire either up or down through the centre of the stem. In this way, it will not be visible, and neither will the stem nor the petal formation be punctured, which would cause the material to dehydrate more rapidly.

FINE SILVER BINDING WIRE is used for fashioning ribbon bows. Make one loop and secure with a twist of silver wire. Make another loop securing it in the same place with the same length of wire. Continue adding loops until the bow is sufficiently full.

FLORAL TAPE is used to cover non-silver wires. There are several varieties obtainable and one should experiment before deciding on any particular brand. It has been known to vary in performance in extreme climates.

Further Equipment

RECEPTACLES It is advisable to keep a few plastic saucers handy which are useful for arranging designs in containers that will not hold water, such as baskets. However, since they have absolutely no decorative appeal, they should be regarded only as receptacles and not containers. They are available in varying sizes, in green, white or black.

FLOWER FOOD is sold either in small packets in powder form or as a liquid essence which must be diluted according to the directions on the bottle. The packets contain enough powder to make about 2 pints of solution. As well as the nourishment, which will noticeably prolong the life of your flowers, the preparation also contains a germ inhibitor specially formulated to keep the water pure.

Bases

A base is a relatively undecorated stand upon which the container holding a flower arrangement is placed. Such bases may by themselves serve to add colour, to give a design visual weight and added texture, to provide further interpretation, and, practically speaking, to raise the design and to protect furniture from water spillage.

Any design that you make should have all its parts in harmony with each other, so avoid putting anything under an arrangement without considering the final effect. As an example, if you were to put a red satin base under a green-dominated landscape arrangement, it would totally lack in harmony, just as placing an elegant arrangement in fine china on a wooden slab would.

From the economic point of view, a base can add interest to your flowers without being too expensive a proposition.

For a simple, attractive base, obtain a set of cake boards in three different sizes; those measuring 6–9in (15–23cm) should give you a good start. Simply take remnants of fabric cut about 1½in (3.8cm) wider than your board all round; make a single hem around your fabric, leaving a small opening to thread through with narrow elastic drawn up to fit the base. You now have a removable cover that you can make up in different colours to go with your arrangement.

The bases can be used separately or in conjunction with one another. Straw table mats and those made of thin cane are useful, and offcuts of hardboard or chipboard can be used after being cut to size and covered with stick-on plastics. The woodgrain, pebble or marble designs are best, since they are compatible with most flowers. Felt can be used for Christmas plaques or special colour bases. Teapot stands, or trivets, can also serve the purpose, and the small round ones with legs can be painted black to resemble Japanese bases.

RIGHT Anthuriums are such dramatic flowers that it is difficult to know what to use them with.
Materials: bowl, pinholder, cane, anthuriums, large ivy leaves.
1 In the pinholder, which is resting in a shallow, water-filled bowl, place the cane at the back and slightly forward. 2 Insert the tallest flower at the back, and bring the next two flowers lower down, framing them with the cane loop. 3 Put the last two flowers lower down in the arrangement. 4 Cover the mechanics with ivy leaves.

ABOVE The container is a painted bleach bottle with a small tin can fitted into the top.
Materials: pinholder, corsage ribbon, homemade black container, small base. Willow loops, hosta leaves, ferns, orchid.
1 Make loops of willow by tying them down with thread, then place them at the back of the pinholder. 2 Add a frame of hosta leaves in the centre of the pinholder. 3 Add the orchid with its ribbon backing to the front of the arrangement, bringing it slightly over the rim of the container. 4 Stand the arrangement on a small base.

LEFT This design makes the most of a beautiful bunch of florist's roses by adding berries, foliage and seedheads to enhance the design.

Materials: tin can with soaked floral-foam filling, base. Privet foliage (Ligustrum ovalifolium), hosta leaves, muscari seedheads, Mahonia japonica berries, Alchemilla mollis, roses.

1 Make a diagonal line of privet, and add hosta leaves at the front. 2 Add seedheads, berries and Alchemilla mollis to the framework, keeping the berries lower in the arrangement. 3 Add the roses, keeping the buds to the top and the sides and the opened roses towards the centre. 4 Place the design to one side of the base.

RIGHT Any assortment from your garden – English or any other nationality – can be used as available.

Materials: two large stones, cotton birds, slate base, tin can with soaked floral foam. Campanula (bellflower), stocks, pontilla, sweet peas, pinks, aquilegia (columbine), scabious, linaria, honeysuckle, hebe, cupressus (cypress), achillea.

1 Using the campanula, start at the top to create an asymmetrical line. 2 Add the mixed flowers to follow the line. Save the heavy flowers for the base. 3 Insert the cupressus at the back and fill in the gaps with hebe and additional cupresses. 4 Place on the base and arrange the stones at one side. 5 Add the cotton birds to complete the picture.

There is a kind of compressed cardboard available at some do-it-yourself shops. This is an excellent material for making bases, as it is about ½in (1.3cm) thick, lightweight and easy to cut. Unfortunately, it is usually only obtainable in large sheets, so you could team up with other flower arrangers to share the cost.

The lids of old cake tins can be covered or painted, and for Christmas designs you can use hardboard or chipboard covered with coloured foil. On the whole, it is better to keep your fabrics plain and matt, as highly patterned or shiny fabric will detract from your flowers.

As for colour, the beginner should stick to mossy and grass greens, browns and greys. The greens blend in with most foliage, the browns are good for dried arrangements, and neutral greys will look good with bright colours combined with grey foliage. As you become more experienced, you can link your bases to the colours of your flowers.

For interpretive arrangments, bases can be cut in irregular shapes and then painted. Boards dotted with glue and sprinkled with sand are ideal for seascapes, and wood slabs or pieces of slate are ideal for landscape arrangements. A good way to make a cheap base for a landscape arrangement is to cut out a piece of hardboard or chipboard in your required size, using an irregular-shaped pattern (experiment with newspaper until you have something you feel is pleasing, then transfer your paper shape to the hardboard, trace it and cut it out with a hacksaw). Mix a small quantity of filler compound and slap over the shape, leaving some areas rough and some smooth. When it is dry, paint with a mixture of blackboard paint and silver paint, which will result in a pewter-grey shade that makes your base look like slate. (It is possible to buy both silver and matt-black paint in model-paint sizes, but since these are such useful colours slightly larger cans are probably cheaper in the long run.)

Other items you could use for bases are small trays, breadboards, rush mats or any plain table mats. Occasionally pieces of marble or glass bases can be bought, which are useful for a change of texture in your collection. Many flower clubs sell flocked or fabric-covered bases in various sizes; cane and rush mats, and wood slabs, are often available from clubs as well.

Background Materials and Accessories

Using long-lasting background material is an economical way of flower arranging. You can employ the leaves of camellia, the swordlike leaves of yucca, and pine and other evergreen foliage, all of which will last a long time. You can then use these backgrounds as a semi-permanent frame for your flowers. Remove the flowers as they go over and replace them with fresh ones. By choosing different flowers each time you can always maintain a fresh look in your arrangements.

Leaves are not the only permanent background that you can use. Dried and glycerined plant material comes in many shapes; these can add interest to a design as well as saving time in arranging. Coconut spathes or palm sheaths are some of the more exotic materials that can make an excellent framework for modern designs.

RIGHT Further useful equipment: *1 Roll of water-resistant satin ribbon about 50 yds (47 m) long. 2 Polypropylene ribbon available in 100 yds (94 m) rolls. 3 A combined pinholder and small container. 4 Candle-cups. 5 and 6 Gold spray and colour spray. When using, it is advisable to wear plastic gloves for protection. 7 Clearlife. Two light coats are better than one generous coat. 8 One of several preparations for spraying on to green leaves to make them shine. 9 Floral tape used to cover wires and to seal the stem-end of support wires. 10 Stub wires, which can be bought in a variety of sizes and thicknesses. 11 Fine silver binding wire.*

Driftwood can always be used – free-standing pieces are easy to replace and give a different look to each arrangement. Branches covered with lichen provide a framework that looks attractive with flowers; and particularly with daffodils or narcissus, as the smooth texture of the flowers contrasts nicely with the rough lichen.

Glycerined beech looks very handsome with orange or yellow chrysanthemums, and the glycerined beech that goes almost black is lovely to use with red flowers.

Ordinary bamboo canes can be cut to different sizes to give a permanent framework for your flowers, and you can experiment with thick basketry cane to make loops and twirls which add interest to designs. Painted plant material is another way of making backgrounds for your flowers; you can paint wood or preserved leaves that are looking a little jaded, and in so doing you can create new and interesting colour combinations.

Metallic car sprays are good to use for pretty colours; mauves, blues, pinks and greens are especially attractive. If you want a disco-type, ultra-modern arrangement, try painting background material with fluorescent poster paints – it's *very* eye-catching!

Accessories are anything that isn't plant material. Most people have objects around the house such as figurines, attractive glassware, glass floats, candles or ornaments of some kind, and, provided they fit happily with your flowers,

you can make much more of your arrangement with them.

A very good way to cut down on the number of flowers you will need is to place a reasonable-sized figurine in front of a small painted tin can, then to work in your flowers around the figurine. This method will save at least three flowers. Place the finished design on a two-tiered base.

Glass floats, available at seaside resorts, can be used effectively in arrangements. They usually come in mauve, green or blue, and if their nets are removed, they can add a sparkling interest to a few flowers. With their nets left on, you can use the floats with a few shells to create a seascape. These look lovely with soft colours of blue-grey, mauve, green and white.

When using an ornament, bear in mind the following tips to help you improve your arrangements. Avoid gimmicky ornaments, such as those with highly coloured patterns and of very shiny china. Try to use the flowers whose colours will blend in with the ornament you are using. You will find that wooden ornaments, along with those made of basketry or straw, combine very well with dried arrangements. Brown pottery blends in well with dried materials.

Keep an eye out for interesting shapes and colours in wine bottles; some are most attractive, especially the pottery or stone wine bottles that you can occasionally buy; these are quite compatible with still-life or kitchen arrangements.

RIGHT Glass, porcelain and plastic containers can all be used effectively.

CONTAINERS

From the beginning of time, containers must have been some of the first domestic 'implements'. For apart from weapons, people had to have receptacles in which to carry and store liquid for drinking and presumably for washing. And what is amazing is that now in the twentieth century, the basic shape is much the same as it was in the days before the Greek and Roman Empires.

To see a contemporary consignment of water and oil jars being unloaded on a busy Greek quayside is to be temporarily transported hundreds of years back in time. How logical in shape these traditional containers are. They are narrow at the neck to prevent evaporation, and at the same time, they are elegantly bulbous (if that is not a contradiction in terms), so that they hold a maximum amount of liquid. Bernard Leach, the father of handmade pottery in England, adopted the classic Greek container as the basis for so many of his designs, which have been copied by his students all over the world.

Formal arrangements were usually contrived with flowering plants set into large containers. Many of these containers were extremely beautiful and we are fortunate that examples have been preserved in mosaics, paintings and tapestries, in stately homes and museums in many countries. It seems as though these objects were designed purely as art forms. Indeed, many of them are so beautiful in their own right that they were never intended to hold flowers – perhaps one shapely branch or a perfect stem of flowers for some very special occasion.

Until the nineteenth century, few cut flowers were used in private homes. It was the fashion among the rich to decorate their homes with pictures of flowers, but of course the ordinary people could not afford pictures and so resorted to the real thing. Vases and containers, though not as ornate as those previously mentioned, were still strictly formal. They were deep, so as to hold plenty of water, and wide, which usually resulted in the arrangement either looking sparse or requiring a huge amount of material to fill it. Certain receptacles in the household were regarded as 'flower vases' and as far as we know, no other vessels were pressed into service.

This situation prevailed almost to the end of the nineteenth century, when interior decoration was at its most opulent. But after the First World War, certain values were dramatically changed. Furnishings became more streamlined, due in no small measure to the lack of domestic help. For many people, this was real liberation – no longer did they have to live with heavy and overbearing 'heirlooms' cluttering small crowded living rooms. Interiors became noticeably less fussy: fabrics were plainer and colours less confused.

Fabrics, wallpaper, furniture and flower vases were produced with a simple handmade style – even then, many of these vases were still too large. Incidentally, the Japanese are expert in designing suitable bases and containers, and some of their smaller ones, with very narrow necks, are perfect for a single flower.

Along with this change in attitude to interior decoration was the upsurge of horticultural interest. However, until the early 1940s, containers, certainly in Britain and America, were still somewhat stylized. Other countries led the way,

notably Germany, Italy and Japan, with new handmade designs created especially for those people newly interested in flower arranging.

Many people have now become more conscious of the innate possibiities of all types of containers, whether they have been specially designed for flowers or not. Indeed, this produces an added challenge since antique shops and the corner 'junk shop' can produce some real treasures in terms of size, shape, finish and general design.

It should be remembered that a collection of vases and containers does not come together overnight and neither is it a good idea to buy too many at one time. They should be collected exactly as one might collect any other *objets d'art:* slowly and objectively.

If you are buying an expensive container, first make sure that you like it, for you will have to live with it; and be sure the colour is something that will blend with plant material. Although white and black are neutral, black doesn't show soft colours to advantage, and unless all-white flowers are to be used, white containers can dominate the flowers.

As to style, it is a good idea to collect different sorts of designs. An open container with a good area inside for water scenes is useful, as is a modern container, perhaps one with two openings that can increase the ways you can use it. Also good to have on hand are a basket with a handle, an attractive box, and a cherub or other figurine-shaped vessel for more formal arrangements. Containers with a pedestal in china or metal are useful, and perhaps one of opaque glass, since its opacity makes it much easier to hide the mechanism.

Other unusual containers may be obtainable from time to time; some have limited use but are fun to experiment with. Antique containers are useful if you enjoy doing period designs, but these can be very expensive.

Other containers which are lovely to own are the spelter (a kind of zinc) figurines which were used for lamps and have been adapted for usage as containers. The arms on these are usually a bit vulnerable, so care should be taken when carrying them from place to place. Marble containers should always have a supplementary container inside, as the damp can spoil them. Silver is easily scratched, so again, a lining of some sort is advisable to prevent this.

With accessories the choice is endless; from plastic figurines, which are inexpensive, to Royal Doulton statuettes, which are much more highly priced, all are suitable.

Anything you enjoy can be used when arranging at home for your own personal pleasure, such as a carved wooden elephant or a china swan; but for shows it must be appropriate to the theme. But in both cases, keep away from the gimmicky and garish, for they will do your flowers no favours.

DIY Containers

Before you do anything rash like spending money, remember that to a flower arranger *any* container that is capable of holding water or floral foam can be pressed into use. There is no need to rush out and buy expensive containers, since there are many things about the house that you can use – jugs, coffee mugs, baking dishes, ashtrays, even that old teapot with a broken lid.

A good way of saving money – and unleashing your creativity – is to have a go at making your own containers. The basic ingredients for doing this are yoghurt cartons, empty tin cans, fabrics, leftover pieces of braid, stick-on plastic, bleach and liquid detergent bottles, paint, glue and other finishing materials.

The easiest container is a simple bleach bottle – cut off the nozzle end, level off the top and paint it. Or, if straight-sided, cover it with glued-on fabric. Cut the fabric about 1in (25mm) larger than the perimeter of the container and glue under ¼in (6mm) on one long side so that this can be stuck on top of the other long side. Finish off the top and bottom with a length of braid.

Bind string around a tin can to give it an interesting texture; you only need to glue the ends. Cover a bleach bottle (one of the smooth, straight ones) with a piece of contact paper or other adhesive-backed plastic material. It will take you all of five minutes to do.

With tall containers that you have made, the simplest form of mechanics is leftover floral foam three-quarters of the way up, and a new piece in the remainder. However, should you wish to use a small pinholder, you will need a small tin can that fits snugly into the top of the container,

then fill the container with made-up filler compound to the bottom of the tin can, making sure that the can is level with the rim of the container. Allow the filler to dry out before putting the tin into the final position. Small plastic containers such as those used for ice cream or cream can be stuck together with a strong glue. Stick them together at their bases (one being upside-down), and when the glue has dried paint in the colour of your choice. If you want, finish off with narrow Russian braid at the top and bottom.

Cans such as the flattish ones that you get pineapple slices in can have split bamboo cut to size and stuck all around its sides.

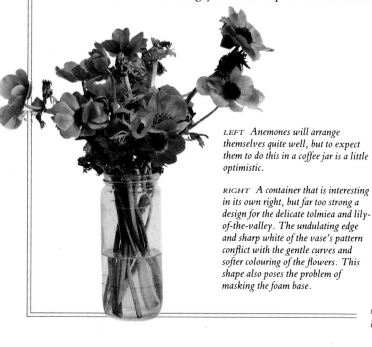

LEFT Anemones will arrange themselves quite well, but to expect them to do this in a coffee jar is a little optimistic.

RIGHT A container that is interesting in its own right, but far too strong a design for the delicate tolmiea and lily-of-the-valley. The undulating edge and sharp white of the vase's pattern conflict with the gentle curves and softer colouring of the flowers. This shape also poses the problem of masking the foam base.

LEFT Vinca major *and stitchwort in a handmade pottery vase produce a lovely, natural arrangement.*

BELOW Any mixture of similar flowers can be used in this pleasing design.
Materials: figurine with screw-on candle-cup filled with soaked floral foam. Box foliage, stocks, sweet peas, spray carnations, roses, scabious.
1 Insert a long piece of the curved box foliage to one side, and shorter piece at the other. 2 Place the sweet peas and spray carnations at the top, making a curved outline. 3 Fill in with the smaller flowers, adding the heavy ones in the middle. 4 Bring some flowers forward over the rim, letting them flow down. 5 Fill in the gap with short flowers and small pieces of foliage.

An urn with grooves can be painted in moss green, its groove lightly touched up with black paint to give it an antique look. Or you an add a tin can the same size as the base of the container, which you can then cover with a remnant of matching velvet and finish with narrow braid.

Shells are another good form of container, and even the smaller ones are fine for dainty arrangements. With most shells a piece of floral foam cut to fit will hold your plant material.

Containers can be made of wood provided you are handy with a saw. However, with wooden containers it is important to remember that they will need a lining of some sort to enable them to hold water.

If you want to add to your collection of containers without spending too much money, go to charity (thrift) shops, jumble (rummage) sales, car boot sales, swap meets, flea markets and junk shops, where you may well be able to find something that you can use, if not an outright treasure. Just make sure that it has a good shape and is in good shape – you can always give the receptacle a coat of paint if you don't like the colour.

PICKING FLOWERS

*I*f you have a garden you can really enjoy yourself with flower arrangements. Not only can you grow what you need, but you can experience the pleasure of watching your garden grow, season after season.

Growing Your Own

If you have a small garden, it is much better to grow any suitable plants that grow well in your area. If you see the plants you want to grow flourishing in neighbours' gardens, they are quite likely to do well in yours. Go for the easier plants rather than those that are difficult to grow, but if you want to experiment with more temperamental specimens, grow them in pots. You can then move them around so that they are subject to favourable growing conditions.

If your garden has a lot of space in it, annuals and half-hardy annuals are a quick way to obtain plant material for picking while you are waiting for the perennials to mature.

Another trick is to grow plants that are not easily obtained at the florist. You could, for example, grow Rembrandt, Viridiflora and lily-flowered tulips, not the more easily bought cottage types. They do not take up any more room, and the bulbs are not that much more expensive than the other, more common kinds, and you will find that you get more interest in your arrangements by doing this.

City dwellers who have a balcony can grow quite a few subjects in tubs or pots. The larger tubs will take quite substantial shrubs, and if you choose an evergreen subject, you will have plant material to pick from even in the winter months. Underplant with small bulbs or annuals.

Wild Plants

So many arrangers are what might be called 'floral snobs', they won't use anything that has not been cultivated, and in doing so miss out on some of the most interesting plant material of all – wild plant material.

Now it should be made quite clear that you must *never* pick anything that is rare. Also, never cut anything that has only a small clump growing. But a lot of wild plants are so numerous that they are almost classed as weeds.

Most wild flowers lose moisture rapidly, and it is advisable to ensure that you have some means of protecting them on the way home. Ideally a bucket of water is the best solution, but failing that, a damp cloth or newspaper wrapped around the stems and kept as cool as possible will give them a good chance of survival. Avoid carrying them, as even the smallest amount of body heat from your hand can make them deteriorate. As soon as you arrive back home, recut the stem ends and give them a long deep drink of cold water before you arrange them.

Many wild flowers produce attractive seedheads. You can use these in the green state, or when they have dried, as additions to your winter flower arrangements.

Buying Flowers In

FLORISTS When buying flowers, go into a florist shop and sniff hard: if you can smell decayed plant material, leave without buying. This is an almost fool-proof guide that the florist is careless about conditioning and looking after his or her flowers.

When you do find a flower shop that smells sweet and clean, then start to inspect the stock. All plant material should look fresh and crisp, and be uncrumpled in appearance. It should look as though it still needed a little time to come out or open up. A good florist will condition his or her more expensive plant material, although it would not be economic to spend a lot of time on the cheap market bunches. The florist will protect the more fragile blooms from extremes of heat and cold, and those placed outside the shop in boxes will be sprayed with water when required.

NURSERIES AND GROWERS These generally specialize in only a few kinds of flowers intended for markets and florists, which means that the flowers must be fresh.

STREET VENDORS Buying flowers from these sources depends a great deal on the characters who are actually selling the flowers. They don't carry such large supplies, and visits to the flower market are usually very frequent. You should get value for money, provided you make sure the material is crisp and fresh.

GREENGROCERS AND GROCERY STORES Some grocers sell flowers as a sideline. If the produce is local, it is usually quite good. However, be careful of the multiple stores, or chains, who are often guilty of dumping boxes of flowers in exposed positions of cold or heat.

GARDEN BUNCHES When out in the country in the summer, you will often see signs outside small gardens offering 'Fresh-cut Flowers'. These are often gardeners selling their suplus stock. Usually presented as mixed bunches they are great for making a variegated flower arrangement, and as the bunches are usually generous, you can make a massed design.

Flowers – And Other Plant Materials

It is important that the flower arranger should learn the value of plant material as distinct from flowers. Although we always refer to the craft as 'flower arranging', it also covers the use of a wide variety of plant material.

Flowers, foliage, fruit, vegetables, berries, seedheads, grasses, lichen, fungi, driftwood, gourds – all of these items can be used in flower arrangements for the home. For example, everyone buys fruit and vegetables for the home. It is not eaten all at once, so why not use the odd apple or pepper to add interest or a different texture to your arrangements?

Grasses can be gathered from the wild; so can berries, lichen, seedheads and driftwood. Even patches of waste ground or road-side verges can yield things like teazles, plantains or dock.

Berries are very colourful items. They include the almost-black elderberries, orange wild rosehips and bittersweet, and wine-red hawthorn berries, to name but a few – all these are to be found in hedgerows and are marvellous for making a few flowers go a long way.

Antirrhinum

Lily

Arum Lily

Broom

Daffodil

TECHNIQUES IN ARRANGEMENT

*Y*our material will presumably come from either the florist's shop, or the garden, or both. In either case, it will need a certain amount of care and attention before being arranged. This is called conditioning.

Conditioning

Garden flowers can be cut in the early morning or late evening. The moment a stem is severed from the parent plant, its life support is cut off. In order that the flower or foliage can continue to survive we compensate by putting it in water, preferably in a flower food solution. At most florists, you can buy a very good powdered product which, when added to the water as instructed, helps flowers to last a long time. Not even this can give it all the nourishment it was getting from the root system, but it will help to prolong its freshness.

Material from the flower shop will already have been conditioned but the stems will callous over in transit and

1

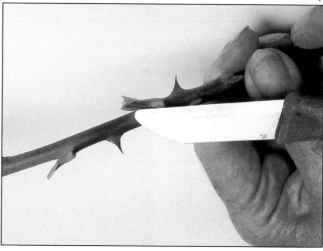

2

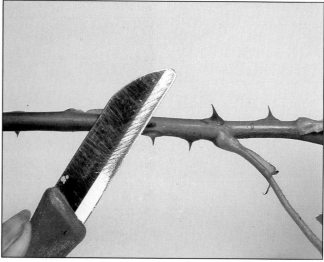

3

ABOVE. Cutting the stem at the conditioning stage. Stems of garden flowers should be cut at a sharp angle and with a sharp knife before being stood in water.

RIGHT. 1 To condition and de-thorn roses take a sharp knife and cut off any leaves which are growing on the lower part of the stem. Remember to work

with the knife blade pointing away from the body. 2 With the blade of your knife almost flat against the stem, carefully remove the thorns at the base of the tem to give about a 5.3in (13cm) length of stem to hold. 3 With the knife blade at the same angle, and facing away from you, slice the remaining thorns off, finishing at the head.

should therefore be re-cut. They can then be treated as flowers from the garden although they will not need to stay as long in the conditioning bucket before being arranged.

To condition our garden material, before cutting prepare a container of water, adding the correct amount of flower food. A deep plastic bucket is the most useful but it need not be completely filled. It has recently been established that most flowers do not, in effect, require deep water, the ideal depth being about 7in (20cm). Bulb-grown flowers are an exception and need only 3–4in (8–10cm). As you cut the flowers, strip off any leaves low down on the stems. Always carry them head downwards as this helps to retain any moisture in the stems. Before standing the material in water, use a very sharp knife and trim each stem end to a sharp point. The exposed angle will offer a larger surface to the water than if the stem were cut straight across.

Any stems carrying thorns, such as roses and some shrubs, should be trimmed, not only for easy handling while you are arranging, but to prevent the thorns from hooking into other flowers. To de-thorn roses, hold your knife blade almost flat against the stem and 'chop' each thorn away. Alternatively, the thorns can be pulled off one by one between finger and thumb but this is a very slow process. Garden roses rarely refuse to take up water. Amongst flowers which may need special attention are lilac, poppies, zinnias and marigolds. Lilac will take up water more readily if most of the foliage is stripped off. It also has very woody stems and prefers to be conditioned in hot water.

Poppies are supposedly very short-lived, but if the stems are instantly plunged into very hot water, or the end is sealed over a flame, they will last for several days. You can sometimes revive florist's roses that start to bend over at the neck by this method. It is also used for clematis and young foliage.

Zinnias and large marigolds sometimes droop their heads just below the flower. The stems are hollow and seem incapable of supporting such magnificent flowers. Insert a wire inside the stem until it reaches the flower-head – this will keep it upright and the flower will take up water happily.

Set your material in a cool, draught-free place to rehabilitate before being arranged. Flowers do not really thrive in direct sunlight, particularly where the heat is concentrated through glass. But it is surprising how tolerant they are once they have been properly conditioned.

An appealing, well-balanced design should ideally include both buds and open flowers. However, a fully matured flower does not have as long a vase life as a younger bud or flower. This should be taken into consideration when planning the arrangement.

Bulb-grown flowers are wonderfully trouble-free, though if they are cut too tight, the flower will never develop.

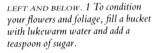

LEFT AND BELOW. 1 To condition your flowers and foliage, fill a bucket with lukewarm water and add a teaspoon of sugar.

2 Strip all lower leaves away from the stem.

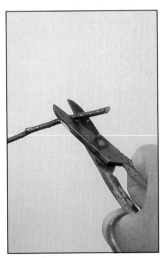

3 Recut the stem and then place in the mild sugar solution for two hours or overnight.

Most shop flowers will have been several hours, indeed even a few days, in transit during which time they have been without water. However, good conditioning will usually 'set them on their feet again', although some flowers, such as roses, occasionally refuse to take up water. In this case, re-cut the stem and stand the rose in hot water. This will soften the stem tissues and the flower will probably take up water within a few moments. Or, stand it in a carbonated liquid such as fizzy lemonade for example. The 'fizz' will drive the liquid up the stem while the sugar content feeds the flower.

Heavy wooded stems such as chrysanthemums, branches of trees, flowering trees and shrubs should, if possible, be broken at the stem end with your fingers. If the branch is too tough to break this way, cut it with secateurs and condition in very hot water.

The concept of hammering hardwood stems to pulverize the end has been rejected on the basis that the 'fringed' stem that results is an ideal breeding ground for bacteria.

While on the subject of bacteria, it is worth pointing out that diseased materials should never be used and that all the containers you use for either conditioning or arranging should be kept perfectly clean. From time to time, they should be sterilized and cleaned thoroughly. Similarly your tools will also need to be cleaned. The blades of knives and scissors should be polished with steel wool and regularly sharpened.

Forcing Flowers and Other Plant Material

In midwinter it is possible to bring some sprays of forsythia indoors to force, even though at this time they resemble little more than knobbly sticks. Choose the stems with plenty of small buds up the sides, then place them in about

Two pieces of gypsophila cut from the same branch being treated with a fixative spray (ABOVE). One of these stems was then placed in a flower food solution, the other in plain water. The benefit gained from the flower food treatment can be seen in the second photograph (RIGHT) taken a week later.

2 inches (5cm) of cold water and stand them in the kitchen window. Change the water frequently so that the stems do not become soggy, and put the ends that have been in water under the cold tap to prevent any build-up of slime.

In a month or two the forsythia are usually in full flower. As soon as they start to show colour, arrange them – and bring indoors another batch. In this way you can have a succession of winter blossoms. In the garden they seldom start to show colour until very late in the winter, so that means you have a whole extra month in which to appreciate the yellow flowers.

You may be able to force the catkins and pussy willow about two to three weeks earlier than they will appear outside, but at that time of the year, when flowers are at their scarcest (and most expensive), it is worth the effort. Pussy willow makes a pretty framework for a few anemones or a bunch of daffodils, and because you can curve it in your hands, you can make outlines for winter moderns. Curve by placing your thumbs under the willow, and then gently pressing down along the stem until the desired arc is obtained.

Preserving Plant Material in Glycerine

Preserving plant material means you always have something on hand to create a flower arrangement. In addition, it may provide striking differences in texture and colour between specimens even of the same plant.

The best-known method preserves plant material in glycerine (glycerol). The recipe is simple, and it results in foliage or seedheads that boast a lovely, silky texture.

You will need one part glycerine to two parts of very hot water, enough to give you about 3–4in (7.5–8cm) of solution in a 1lb (.45kg) glass jar (make up a teacupful to get this amount). Mix thoroughly, then take your branch of leaves, cut the end off the branch and place it in the solution. All leaves that are insect-nibbled should be cut away, as well as any leaves that have holes in them or are otherwise damaged. Seedheads such as foxgloves, dock and plantains can all be preserved in this way. Most foliage will take up the solution well, with beech being just about the best type of leaf you can use.

Beech has the added advantage of being one of the quickest foliages to take. It is possible to preserve beech in four days in a warm kitchen.

Grasses can also be preserved by this method, and it is particularly good for pampas grass, which retains its lovely, soft texture when dry.

ABOVE *A popular method of preserving is to immerse plant material in a solution of one part glycerine to two parts water.*

LEFT *This small design is suitable for the top of a bookcase or a coffee table. It could also be used as a table decoration.*
Materials: painted tin can filled with soaked floral foam, oval base. Roses, spray carnations, Alchemilla mollis.
1 Begin with the rosebuds to form a low outline. 2 Add the carnations and Alchemilla mollis. 3 Bring the fuller flowers toward the centre. 4 Fill in the gaps with alchemilla and its foliage, along with a few more leaves. 5 Place on the base.

Holding and Fixing

A successful flower arrangement depends on how firmly it is anchored to the base. There are several methods of preparing containers and bases; floral foam is now so much a part of the flower arranger's basic equipment that it is difficult to remember how we ever made an arrangement without it. But, efficient though it is, it is certainly not the only way of supporting the material: in fact, some flowers prefer to be directly in water whenever possible. Proteas, in particular, last far longer if they can stand in deep water, while gladioli, although they last quite well when arranged in foam, really prefer to have their stems in water.

Wire mesh, pinholders, moss, sand and cut branches all help to support the material and your choice of method must be dictated by the size and type of design, as well as the material being used.

Many arrangers like to use mesh as well as foam. This is a very valid method. particularly for rather large heavy material. Mesh used alone should be crumpled to fit the shape of the container, preferably with some left well above the rim. If you press it in too low, you will have no support for your lateral stems. Even though it may seem fairly firm, it is advisable to secure it to the rim of the container with adhesive tape or string.

If you are using a container with an extremely high glaze, or made of glass, the Oasis-fix will not adhere firmly enough. The solution is to fold a piece of tissue or paper kitchen towel and use it as a small non-skid mat for the foam. The block should then be fixed firmly with sellotape.

Sand is sometimes used at the base of a container for dried flowers. But be very careful, for sand is heavy and if too much is used, it could make the base of the vase fall out.

If you are totally without any support mechanism, cut some stems or small branches to the depth of the vase. Almost fill the aperture and they will give the necessary support, though a design with spreading lateral lines would not be practical.

In deciding the size of foam, the main thing to remember is that once you have inserted a stem you have made a hole

RIGHT An old-fashioned wire support in a wide-mouthed urn. Both support and urn pose problems; the urn requires a very large number of flowers for a balanced design, and the wire support (superseded by more modern floral foam and mesh) is very difficult to handle. Definitely a container to leave well alone.

BELOW LEFT Soaked floral foam will need to be secured to a shallow 'open' base. It can be impaled on prongs which have been attached to a plastic saucer by Oasis-fix. Both prongs and container must be clean and dry if the Oasis-fix is to adhere firmly.

BELOW RIGHT A foam base should stand at least 1in (2cm) above the rim of your container. Deep bowls may need two pieces of foam stacked to achieve sufficient height. A second smaller piece may be impaled on the first and the two secured firmly to the container with adhesive tape.

It is important to cut soaked foam to a size that will fit securely into the neck of your container. A square piece should be wedged into a round neck and a round piece into a square neck. This ensures a good fit and leaves room for adding more water when necessary.

A large pot of this kind (RIGHT) can be made smaller by inserting a smaller pot into its neck. This solves the problem of securing the foam sufficiently well to carry a big design. It also reduces the amount of water – and therefore of additional weight – needed to keep the flowers and foliage fresh.

BELOW Mesh is particularly useful as extra support for heavy designs. It should be fixed to your container with a loop of adhesive tape secured on either side. With a large container, the mesh may need to be secured in three places.

LEFT *For this contemporary free-style arrangement a large pinholder is sufficiently heavy to sit firmly in the shallow highly-glazed dish. The decorative stones help to mask the pinholder so that the minimum of foliage is needed. Each stem should be held very close to the pinholder and impaled firmly (*BELOW*).*

Large containers, of course, present a greater challenge than smaller ones. For example, the type of brass container sometimes used in churches becomes impossibly heavy if filled with water, while the neck is often rather small. One solution to the problem is to locate a smaller container that will effectively slot into the neck thus forming a kind of inner lining. Alternatively, a large candle-cup may be used, though even the largest size may not be big enough to hold a piece of foam large enough to support a really large design.

Each time you make an arrangement, try to keep the size of foam used, down to a minimum. Although it is far easier to design into a large block, it needs a lot of material to mask it which is, at least, time-consuming. But never make it so small as to risk the foam collapsing. Like many other skills, there are certain guidelines to follow, but eventually, one becomes experienced in what your tools – in this case, the foam – can do for you.

Remember, before you begin a design, to add water to the container as soon as you are satisfied that the base is firm. It is far easier at this stage than when all the material is in place.

In order to travel with a design, it is safer to pour the water out when the arrangement is finished, and take a small can with you to refill the container once it is in place. The well-soaked foam will keep the flowers fresh for many hours but in a warm atmosphere you will get a longer vase life from the flowers if the container is kept filled.

which obviously weakens the block. If you have never used foam, cut a piece you feel will take every stem comfortably. If your container has a round opening then choose a square piece of foam, and vice versa. This allows for a better fit and there will be a space left to insert the spout of the watering can for adding more water.

The depth of the foam is easier to estimate. Since most arrangements have some lateral stems, make sure the foam stands at least 1in (2cm) above the rim of the container otherwise you will be trying to insert stems into mid-air.

Pinholders of varying sizes are useful for shallow containers. They are very heavy and need no fixative to hold them in position. They can also be used together with wire mesh for larger arrangements that include heavy branches and flowers with large stems, for example, arum lilies. They will also tolerate foam, but prefer to be directly in water.

A few more pieces of foliage to cover the broom stems would have improved the design.

Materials: *jug, wire mesh. Broom, skimmia foliage, wallflowers* (Cheiranthus *species, or gillyflower), tulips, chaenomeles (flowering quince).*

1 Measure the wire mesh about 1½ times the circumference of the jug. Crumple the wire up, leaving the cut ends at the top; insert the wire into the jug. Add water. 2 Add broom, twisting the cut ends of the wire around it to help hold it in position. Insert a piece of foliage to cover the rim. 3 Add the wallflowers, following the curve of the design. 4 Place the tulips in position, still following the basic line. Add chaenomeles and a few more wallflowers to fill in the gaps.

Foliage: Special Considerations

Foliage is lovely in its own right, and an arrangement of leaves and stems can be just as colourful and pretty as one of flowers. New arrangers tend to think of foliage only as green, but when they start to look around them – in nature, as well as at florists – they can see the different shades and patterns available.

Rhus and copper beech produce bronze foliage; privet and gold-heart ivy bear yellow foliage; santolina and *Stachys lanata* (or lamb's-ears) leaves are grey, and there are myriad varieties of leaves in green and white. Add to this your glycerined foliage, which gives you brown, beige and reddish-browns, and you have greatly increased the spectrum of colours available. There are more subtle tones as well, like the blue-grey of rue and some of pines. An especially colourful example is a berberis that is purple splashed with pink; and think of the familiar, showy leaves of coleus and of some of the geraniums.

Autumn hues give us yellow, reds and orange, and although they don't last all that long, such autumn foliage can make a beautiful arrangement.

Foliage should, of course, be selected with as much care as flowers, keeping an eye on colour, shape and texture.

Most leaves condition well by being submerged for several hours in clear water. Examples that respond well to this technique are hosta, begonia rex and chlorophytum. Those leaves with a hairy or velvety texture should not be submerged but should be stood in shallow water. Green foliage should be laid flat in a bath or basin and given a good soak. Yellow foliage requires a slightly different method. Just strip the foliage and stand it in cold water after recutting the stem end. If yellow foliage comes into contact with cold water it will turn brown, so this is something you do *not* soak.

The leaves of grey foliage should be wrapped in a cloth with just the stem ends showing. Place them in boiling water and hold them there for about 20 seconds. Then put the ends in cold water. Some grey foliage with feltlike leaves can, if wet, siphon water out of a container, so keep as much of the surface of the leaves as dry as possible.

Young leaves are quite charming, with their fresh green shapes, but unfortunately they do not last very long. Some, however, will enjoy being stood in a few inches of quite hot water, to which flower food has been added.

Foliage is interesting when strong shapes are used together in a single arrangement. Matt yucca foliage and shiny fatsia leaves, for example, look attractive, perhaps arranged along with some apples (place the fruit on sticks to give them a little height). Foliage and wood are another combination that you could consider; chunky wood with foliage for

ABOVE *The wonderful hues of autumnal foliage will donate rich browns, reds and golds to a pure foliage arrangement.*

BELOW *Create variety in an all-green foliage design by emphasizing the varied shape and texture of the leaves.*

height and heavy leaves at the base can give you a quick and pleasing design.

When you do have a good selection of foliage, treat it as you would flowers. You can make a background with something ordinary like green privet, adding your more colourful foliage to the front of the design.

Foliage showing fat buds can also be forced. Hawthorn, one of the first to come out, has pretty leaves that nicely complement spring flowers. When the forsythia you have forced (see page 34) has finished flowering, you can take off the spent flowers and let the leaves develop, again providing attractive foliage for your spring arrangements.

BELOW LEFT The delicately shaded green and cream vase with its slender neck is an obvious choice for a green arrangement. The bell-like flowers of the tolmiea make an interesting contrast with the deep red fingers of the hellebore leaves and the feathery, downward-curving hedge parsley.
BELOW CENTRE Further contrast has been added at the centre of the design on the left with the addition of hellebore flowers and the still-green flowers of the Viburnum opulus or snowball tree.
BELOW RIGHT A third alternative. The hellebore flowers and Viburnum opulus have gone, and the deep red of the hellebore foliage is given prominence once more. Below, new contrast is provided with the introduction of four types of variegated leaf.

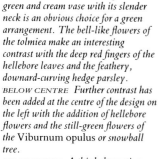

The material (LEFT) chosen for a green arrangement is not strictly foliage alone since the seed heads of some bluebells have been included to vary texture.

Using these simple materials this arrangement (ABOVE) has been designed for all-round effect, with grasses forming a central line.

A E S T H E T I C
P R I N C I P L E S

*B*efore we take a look in closer detail at some of these stylistic elements it might be useful to provide a brief list of relevant factors and terms in the form of a glossary. Most – if not all – of these elements should be considered before and during the creation of a flower arrangement.

General Notes on Style

BALANCE An arrangement is balanced when the visual weight on each side of an imaginary vertical line through the middle of the arrangement is equal. The design should not appear to tilt backwards or forwards or to the left or the right. The design should not be top-heavy, since the focal area is low in the design.

Darker colours should be used low down near the middle. Place the thinner pieces of material at the top and the outside of the design, and the heaviest flowers in the centre.

A base can help to give you visual weight, as well as counteract any tendency to heaviness.

CENTRE OF INTEREST The focal area should be under the tallest placement. Round shapes or the most interesting or vivid colours, are useful as a focal point.

Use the larger leaves closest to the middle to bring the eye to the focal point.

All lines should converge at the focal point.

Except for the sparse line designs, there should be a density at the focal point.

CONTRASTS These can be obtained by colour, shape or texture.

DOMINANCE The dominant area in most arrangements is the focal point; a dominant idea can also be used as a theme. Dominant lines, movement, colour or flowers can also be employed.

GRADUATION The graduation of plant material means going from fine to medium to heavy.

HARMONY This can be achieved by:

The repetition of material.

Using plant material that grows naturally in similar conditions.

The use of colour blending.

Employing contrasts such as rough and smooth, light and dark.

Selecting correct containers or bases for your flowers.

PROPORTION This is the relation of size and shape to each other.

The height of the plant material should be approximately 1½–2 times the largest dimension of the container or base. In a horizontal arrangement, the proportion should be about 2–4 times the width or length of the container. In a so-called Hogarth curve the proportions should be two-thirds above the container and one-third below.

An example of bad proportion would be an arrangement wherein the height and width of the plant material are equal.

RHYTHM Use curved containers with curved plant material, and more angular containers with straight plant material.

Prune out any crossing lines.

Place all the stems close together on your mechanics so that they appear to be springing out from one point.

Use any drapes to follow the line of the arrangement.

SCALE (in relation to size only). The size of your plant material should be relative to your container.

The size of the arrangement should be compatible with the room in which it is set up and should be considered vis-à-vis the furniture around it.

The size of individual flowers within an arrangement should be no more than a third to a quarter of the size of their container. Accessories should be no more than about ⅛ to 1/16 of the size of an arrangement, to avoid their dominating the plant material.

TEXTURE This is the surface structure that can be assessed by touch or sight; you can have rough, smooth, dull, shiny, velvety and so on.

If you want to increase the importance of a focal area, a few shiny leaves will make it more obvious. In single-colour designs, various textures can add interest to the arrangement.

In dried designs, a few shiny glycerine-preserved leaves can add spice to the long-life flowers.

Remember that shiny surfaces reflect the light and dull surfaces break up the light particles.

VARIATION Use a variety of shapes, colours and textures.

FAR LEFT Ferns and foxgloves: these are often found on the fringes of woodlands. The container is homemade; it was a large, old-fashioned meat dish bought at a jumble sale.

Materials: *large container, pinholder. Male fern (Dryopteris Filix-mas), foxgloves (Digitalis purpurea), moss.*

1 Make a background of ferns on the pinholder, with the tallest at the back. 2 Add the tallest foxglove near the tallest fern. 3 Cut the other foxglove to different lengths, bringing some slightly to the front with the shorter fern. 4 Use a little moss to hide any mechanism. 5 Fill the container with water.

LEFT This design makes the most of three agapanthus; even the stems are used to assist in the design. Some of the acuba foliage has been pruned off the larger leaves to give a better line.

Materials: *tall brown and lime-green container, soaked floral foam. Acuba foliage, agapanthus. No base is needed for this design.*

1 Place a long stem of trimmed acuba in the centre of the foam, which has been put into the container. Add short pieces, bringing them to the front. 2 Cut the agapanthus to different lengths. Add the cut portions of the stems at the back and to one side. 3 Put in the three agapanthus – two at the back and the shorter one to the front.

RIGHT Gladioli with cork rings.

Materials: *three-opening container, tile on fabric-covered base, three cork rings, soaked floral foam. Gladioli and their leaves.*

1 Cut the three gladioli to different lengths with the most opened stem of flowers cut short. Place this flower in the lowest opening. Place the other flowers in the two other openings, adding a leaf and one looped leaf in the second opening. 2 Loop a leaf in the lower opening with the most opened flower, together with another leaf. 3 Stand on the base, then place the joined cork in front, and the single piece at the back.

The Four Basic Designs

There are four classic design forms used by flower arrangers; they are: the horizontal arrangements, the vertical arrangement, the symmetrical arrangement and the asymmetrical arrangement. The materials you have at hand and where you decide to place your arrangement, will determine the form you choose to work from.

The history of flower arranging dates back to ancient times and all kinds of patterns and forms have evolved through the ages, mainly under the influence of the West and the Far East. The Japanese, for example, have practised the art for well over a thousand years and they are renowned for their pure classic asymmetrical designs. Then there are the Byzantine floral mosaics in Ravenna with their tall symmetrical designs, the stylized Dutch and Flemish flower paintings of the seventeenth and eighteenth centuries, and the proliferation of books and magazines on the art of flower arranging in Victorian times. Definite rules of arrangement, however, were established during this century.

The Horizontal Form

It is usual when making a horizontal arrangement to establish the spread of the design first. Fix these two lines first and then decide the height and depth and work within this framework.

While too many rigid rules and regulations can be stultifying to progress, some of the most obvious rules do make sense. For example, most basket shapes would suggest a horizontal arrangement and that the handle should be left free from encompassing foliage so that it is easy to hold. On the other hand, there may be instances where the designer might feel it necessary to place a few tall flowers above the handle. However, in order to break the rules, one must first learn to apply them.

Arrangements with a horizontal emphasis are particularly suitable for 'window-dressing' an empty fireplace in summer, or a mantelshelf, particularly in a fairly small room where a tall design might otherwise be overpowering.

Arrangements for the dining table whether at home or at a banquet are usually horizontal otherwise no one would be able to see or be seen. The maximum width of such designs is crucial, for there must be ample space for the guests to eat or, in the case of a banquet, speakers' notes and microphones. Graceful and near-symmetrical horizontal designs, sometimes joined with ribbons or ropes of green foliage can effectively enhance what might otherwise be a rather stark dining table.

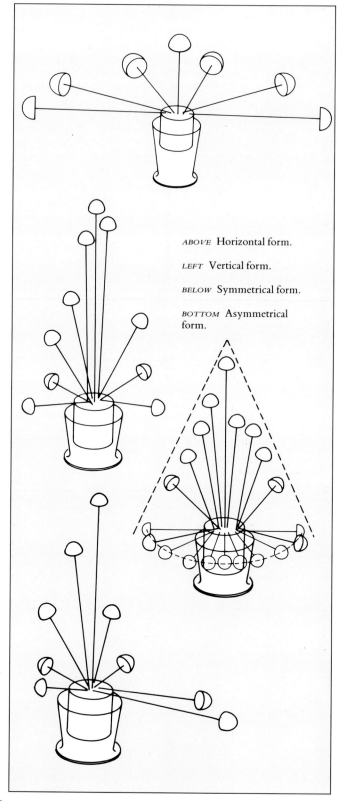

ABOVE Horizontal form.

LEFT Vertical form.

BELOW Symmetrical form.

BOTTOM Asymmetrical form.

*1 To make a horizontal design, 1
first decide on the colour and texture of
your design and gather your materials
together. Here the yellow and orange
of the flowers pick up the colouring of
the foliage at the centre. 2 Cut well-
soaked floral foam so that it fits the
container you have chosen. 3 Not
every design need be constructed from
the outside inwards. Begin in the
middle of this design, masking the foam
with foliage and roughly describing the
shape intended. 4 Now insert your line
flowers. 5 Strengthen the lines with
the addition of more flowers, being
careful not to overcrowd the
arrangement*

The Vertical Form

A simple description of vertical is that the line is at right angles to the horizon. If one then translates horizon into container-rim, it will give a good idea of how material should be set in place. However, most things turn out better if a plan of action is followed and a flower arrangement ought, in effect, to begin with a plan, based on a logical framework.

ABOVE Straight-stemmed flowers like the gerbera are particularly suited to vertical designs. The gerbera may curve, but wiring will ensure that the flower remains upright.

1

2

1 To wire a flower, insert a piece of wire of the correct thickness downwards through the centre of the flower stem into the middle of the flower head.

2 Press the wire gently but firmly back into the centre of the flower with the blade of your knife. Care is needed to ensure the flower remains undamaged.

For this symmetrical arrangement the base is first masked with green hellebore (TOP LEFT) before the three main lines are set in place (BOTTOM LEFT).

Notice (LEFT) how the third flower down to the right of the centre has been placed so as to avoid too formal an effect.

First establish whether the arrangement is to be a facing design – that is, viewed from the front only – or an all-round design. This affects the position of the first main stem. For a facing design, the main line must be set in towards the back of the foam, and for an all-round arrangement, it should be set in the centre of the foam.

The main line should be straight and definitive, and establish the maximum height of the arrangement. Then, two or three more lines should be inserted very close to the first one and parallel to it, each one slightly shorter than the previous one. These will emphasize the main line and help to make it visually stronger.

The next decision is to determine the maximum width of the design. For a facing arrangement, insert two lateral stems aiming towards the position where the main line was inserted.

For an all-round design, insert five stems of equal length radiating from the central line.

All that remains to be done is to add further material at intervals, keeping within your established framework. Take care not to crowd the material – it is always better to have too little rather than too much.

The Symmetrical Form

As few flowers are identical, it is not easy to achieve perfect symmetry with living material. Therefore, an arranger is not expected to measure the two sections exactly for height, width and depth. Your design should rather appear to be symmetrical, giving a satisfying visual balance, bearing in mind, of course, that the basic disciplines should be respected. If your lines are well-placed and the materials carefully chosen, then successful results should follow. A simple arrangement can be made by placing an even number of stems at either side of the central stem.

In choosing the material it is probably easier to get a satisfactory result if you use not more than three types of flower, that is, flowers of differing shapes and sizes, such as delphiniums, roses and spray chrysanthemums. Apart from the type of flower and colour, the classic 'recipe' includes line flowers, which are the materials that give gradation, normally with buds and semi-open flowers, plus materials for emphasis. These are usually mature blooms, often of a strong, clear colour and shape.

Your choice of colour will naturally play an important role in determining symmetry. You may, in fact, make a design which is entirely symmetrical from the point of view of line, yet if the colour values are off-balance, it will never appear to be symmetrical. Do not let this deter you from making symmetrical arrangements.

ABOVE This design is an easy one for a beginner to tackle. Any medium-sized leaves could be used for the backing.

Materials: narrow pot, filled with soaked floral foam, tile base. Five irises, four ivy leaves.

1 Insert an iris bud at the top, and two more lower down, on slightly different levels. 2 Add the last two irises with the lowest one coming over the rim of the container. 3 Back this with ivy leaves, which will hide the mechanics.

The Asymmetrical Form

This form of design is the reverse of the symmetrical type – which is, that each side should be different, possibly in content and certainly from the point of view of line and emphasis.

However, as with the other forms, it needs a firm framework on which to build. So although the main line may not necessarily be set into the middle of the arrangement, it must be seen to be the main line that runs straight into the centre of the design.

Asymmetrical arrangements can also be set vertically or horizontally, but care should be taken so that they are not confused with free-style designs.

However, try not to become intimidated by too many definitions, rules and regulations. These few pointers are intended to help and not to confuse. When you are making an arrangement, imagine, in essence, that the framework is made up of bare twigs which you will then 'dress' with flowers and foliage. Keep the basic structure simple and well-defined to ensure a successful arrangement.

Balance

In flower arranging both balance and proportion, like colour values, are largely a matter for the individual eye. However, one cannot escape the fact that actual balance is needed for the design to be stable. It will either balance or fall over – it is as simple as that. It may seem impossible for arrangements to collapse and overbalance, but they do, with very disappointing results. Fortunately there are several technical ways of preventing this.

It may clarify the situation to pinpoint one or two problem areas. The first one is the size of the foam block. The size needed is most difficult to resolve, since everyone works differently. But before cutting your foam, decide what kind of material you plan to use. If it includes heavy, woody stems, or thick-stemmed flowers such as gladioli and delphiniums for example, or heavy blooms such as chrysanthemums and dahlias, then you will need a fairly large and deep piece of foam. It should be remembered that every time a stem is driven into a block of foam it makes a hole exactly the size of the stem. So if you begin without a clear plan and have to change the position of the stems many times, the block is weakened still further.

In most cases, you may use only one or two chunky stems with quite delicate flowers such as spray carnations, candytuft and other lightweight annuals, or even spray chrysanthemums.

White jug and flowers in the first stages of preparation (TOP). Foam is wedged into the neck and the main lines are set in place. Notice the small but very definite bud carnations describing the structure.

At the next stage (LEFT), existing lines are strengthened with more flowers and some foliage is inserted. The main lines are now to some extent masked.

BELOW Pink carnations would be rather bland, so a little red alstroemeria is added. Notice how the main structure is kept, while at the same time flowers and foliage are added.

In deciding the depth of the foam, you will soon see, with a little experience, when a deeper block is required. For instance, a horizontal arrangement will need more than a vertical design.

When all the foregoing points have been sorted out in your own mind, and really it only takes a moment or two, your next step is to make absolutely sure that the foam block is going to remain firm in its seating. Where practical, use an Oasis-prong plus adhesive tape wrapped around at least twice. When it comes to tackling the design, it is a good idea, if you are not too sure of your plan, to 'sketch' the lines out on the table with some of the material. Or, you could even work into an old piece of foam as a practice run.

The pedestal is probably the type of design that gives the most difficulty where actual balance is concerned. Begin by placing your material right at the back of the foam. To make it safe, put your point of balance two-thirds towards the back of the foam inserting only a few stems into the front portion.

Visual balance is affected or influenced as much by the colour, size, shape and texture of the material, as the way in which it is used.

One of the best critics of any arrangement is a camera lens, for one's eye can see what one intends it to see, which is not always what is recorded by the camera. So, whenever possible, take pictures of your designs, aiming the lens exactly at the centre of the arrangement.

Proportion

Proportion should be seen in every aspect of the design, including the materials used, the proportion of the complete design in relation to the container, and the relationship of the chosen design with its environment.

While varying sizes of material can be used to create a good design, they should be selected with care so that they blend together. Thus, an arrangement of gerbera and freesia might be out of proportion. Even the masking and support foliage can sometimes upset good proportion. When using delicate flowers, such as freesias or Singapore orchids, the foliage should not be too large or heavy from the point of view of colour or texture. However, problems of bad proportion regarding the use of materials are, happily, few and far between. On the other hand, the choice of container is sometimes in error, for it may be too large or too small for the material. This fault is easily corrected by substituting another container.

IMMEDIATE LEFT A well-balanced arrangement of freesias in this chalice type vase. But be warned – a wide-mouthed container like this demands many flowers if a satisfying design is to be achieved.

FAR LEFT This old-fashioned type of kitchen jar has become very popular and they can be used most successfully to complement modern interiors. The polyanthus are visually heavy enough here, but cowslips are too delicate.

BELOW LEFT This handmade pot with its 'Celtic' pattern is an excellent choice for dried flowers. However, flower and design are both wrong here – the dried molucella is not only off-balance but too long for the vase.

Colour: the Colour Wheel

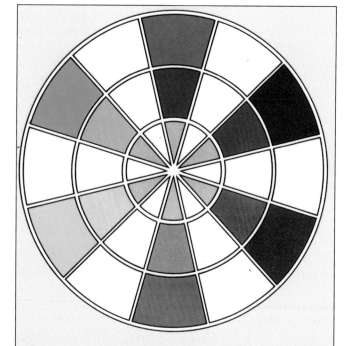

The outer colour wheel shows the three primary colours, yellow, red and blue, from which all others can be made, with secondary colours (pure hues) in between. The middle band shows lighter tints of the same colours and the inner band shows darker shades. The wheel diagrams below illustrate the four basic colour schemes.

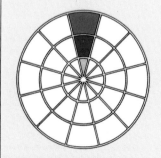

Monochromatic *Shades and tints of any one single colour.*

Harmonic *Groups of any three or four colours lying next to each other.*

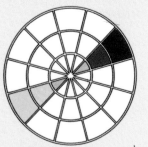

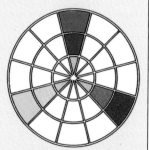

Complementary *Colours which lie opposite each other.*

Triadic *Any three colours lying at equidistant intervals.*

Colour is an important factor in flower arranging. Not only can it create moods, link up with furnishings and help to interpret a theme at a flower show, but it can also make a personal statement, vis-à-vis the continued use of a favourite shade.

In addition to having a specific total value, each colour is said to have a connotation related to human reaction. Thus red is positive and signifies power. Blue is the most introvert colour and implies faith and sometimes meekness, even timidity. Orange is supposed to suggest pride in the nicest sense of the word, while violet denotes gentleness and piety. Green indicates sympathy and compassion, while white is the very essence of light and signifies purity.

Artists and flower arrangers often use a colour wheel to help them understand colour combinations. However, you must remember that this can only be used as a guideline, for flower arrangers cannot mix their colours like artists or decorators. Flowers have subtle shadings, stripes or blotches, as well as stems, stamens and foliage, all of which may be of a different colour.

The first step is to clarify the primary colours: they are red, yellow and blue. All other colours are made from these in varying degrees of intensity. The primaries can be mixed to produce secondary colours, for example, blue and red make violet, yellow and blue make green, while yellow mixed with red produces orange. When black is added to a colour, the result is a shade. When white is added, a tint is obtained. The addition of black or white creates different colours – red, for example, becomes pink with the admixture of white, whereas black added to yellow gives olive green. White, black and grey are considered neutral colours; hue is the pure form of primary, secondary and tertiary colours, and tones are colours that are greyed.

You may wonder what this has to do with flower arranging since we cannot stir a yellow daffodil and a scarlet tulip together in a bowl and produce an orange lily. In flower arrangement it is a question of understanding the values of each colour we use in order to produce the effect we want. For example, a vase with seven scarlet tulips and three pale blue irises would not be at all impressive or interesting, as red is an extrovert dominant colour while blue is receding and gentle. In short, the irises would be totally swamped by the red flowers.

Undoubtedly, colour has a definite effect on our senses, so it is worth remembering that bright striking effects can be made by using warm colours, such as red, orange and warm yellows (these are the advancing colours), while more soothing and delicate designs can be made by using cooler blue-pinks, mauves, blue and purple (these are the receding colours). Grey foliage can also be used in cooler arrangements.

An arrangement with varying levels of one colour, such as pale pink through to red, is described as being mono-chromatic. This category of colour harmony is usually very restful on the eye.

To choose any three neighbouring colours on the colour wheel, for example, from pink through red to mauve, will give you a harmonic colour scheme. In terms of flowers, this type of colour scheme is very pleasing indeed.

For a more striking effect, experiment with complement-ary colour schemes. These are the colours that are directly opposite each other on the colour wheel, such as violet and yellow, blue and orange or green and scarlet. Do not neces-sarily choose the basic hue, but try to use tints and tones of each one. If you use them in well-balanced proportions you will produce very agreeable results.

One point to bear in mind with regard to colour in relation to living flowers is that their colours do change slightly every day. As the flower dehydrates, so the colour drains from it.

Lighting is very important in flower arranging – the colours of both flowers and foliage will look quite different if the arrangement is placed in a dark corner or on a window sill or if it is seen under different types of electric light. Blue and mauve for instance, lose the crisp, clear colour that natural light gives them and become a rather dull grey under electric light. Fluorescent lighting, on the other hand, will enhance blue though it will make red appear a muddy brown. Tungsten lighting is appropriate for red, orange and yellow.

The correct colour, form and texture will also give shape to a design. Colour perspective is built up by graduating and complementing the tonal value of each local colour. Light colours will stand out and become the focal point in your arrangement if you place material of a deeper tonal value behind them. Similarly you can use local colour that has lighter tones to soften and enhance colours that have darker tones.

The subtle use of local colour to create perspective in flower arranging is closely allied to techniques used by artists to give perspective to their paintings.

ABOVE *This tall container makes a lovely base for deep blue/mauve irises, pale mauve honesty flowers and pinky mauve freesias. The straight stems of the irises are set in symmetrically, while the honesty sprays provide a softer outline in contrast.*

ABOVE *Too much of one type of material can be overwhelming. A vertical arrangement consisting of two varieties of lemon and yellow spray chrysanthemums needs another texture and colour to spice it up.*

LEFT *A charming old-world jug with a bouquet of anemones on the front is the obvious container for these long-stemmed anemones. It is quite a luxury to find these flowers with such long stems, so the design was contrived to use as much of the stem and its natural curve as possible. These are arranged in a block of foam, which fits neatly into the neck of the jug.*

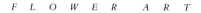

Harmony

In flower arranging, harmony is almost as complex as it is in music. and 'that which forms a consistent or agreeable whole' must be our objective. We must not only use flowers and foliage that are in harmony from the point of view of colour, form and texture, but also in respect of the character of the material. Yes, flowers do have character: compare an arum lily with a violet; a daffodil with a rose.

The material must also harmonize with its container and its surroundings. For instance, a severe-line arrangement based in a wonderful silver dish intended as decoration for a brick fireplace in a sixteenth-century country cottage would not be in keeping with the background. A more simple style of design arranged in a copper or basketware container would be more in harmony with these rustic surroundings.

But always remember that in flower arranging, as in music, enjoyment of the end-products is the main aim, so do not be worried if your concept of harmony does not agree with other people's.

Monochromatic Arrangements

Mono means one, thus a monochromatic arrangement is a design of one colour only. First decide on the colour and then introduce all available tints and shades of the basic colour.

They may be flowers of the same family, but they might also be varied, which would introduce a contrast in texture as well.

Monochromatic harmony is probably the most soothing of all colour combinations, for the eye and mind are not assailed by possibly conflicting tints. Such arrangements are obviously very acceptable in hospitals or in any situation where a calm atmosphere should be preserved. The colour chosen should also be appropriate to the situation. For example, to take a bouquet of red carnations to someone who is ill in an attempt 'to cheer him up' will probably have the reverse effect, while deep pink or a soft clover colour might achieve success. Colour is a continually absorbing aspect of flower arranging and every combination presents both its problems and challenges.

Here sharp colour contrasts emphasize the tonal value and details of the carnation.

Contrast between black and white is strong and makes the white flower stand out.

Similar tones of flower and background colours emphasize the yellow in the petals.

LEFT *Delphiniums are obvious flowers for monochromatic treatment as well as for perpendicular designs. They range from the palest blue to a really rich ultramarine, here underlined by the blue of the glass container. Foliage of contrasting shapes completes the arrangement.*

FAR LEFT *The colour scheme is tints, tones and shades of yellow, and the objective was to capture the curving stem of the Spanish broom.*

Materials: bottle filled with yellow food colouring and water, candle-cup with soaked floral foam taped to bottle, one deep yellow base, one medium yellow base. Spanish broom (Sparticum junceum), chrysanthemums, small ivy leaves.

1 Use the Spanish broom to give a gently curving outline. 2 Place the chrysanthemums over the rim, along with the broom and the ivy leaves. Use the leaves to frame the central flower and to hide the mechanics.

This green has a lighter tonal value than the second and creates a nearer image.

Here, the darker tone of green creates depth and the flower also recedes.

Green appears to emphasize the colour and contours of the carnation.

Detail and contrast are reduced because the tonal values are too similar.

The blue background recedes from the vibrant red carnation.

The yellow and red are both advancing colours with similar tonal values.

The vertical design of arum lilies
(TOP) is a little unimaginative in this
whitemilk glass container, and the
texture of the flowers is very similar to
the finish of the vase. RIGHT Add five
stems of column stock and a contrast in
colour, form and texture is immediately
introduced. This may prove too strong
a contrast for some tastes, so several
heads of lilac are added at the heart of
the arrangement, providing a third
variation in colour value and texture.
ABOVE Close-up of lily and column
stock.

Colour Grouping

Any material that has been grouped together becomes more significant than if it were scattered.

One of the main points in grouping colours is to know where to place certain colours to give the best effect in both the design and its location. Lighter colours can be used as highlights or focal interest, while darker colours can be used to give depth, or to accentuate lighter colours. Most colours are usually more lively if they are not grouped too evenly throughout an arrangement. Think of the design as if you were painting it. 'Paint in' one group of material at a time, leaving one or two stems for the finishing touches.

Contrasts

The term 'contrast' in the art of flower arranging, refers not only to colour, but also to form, texture and the individual character of the material. This means that you could have a design in monochromatic colours combined with contrasting shapes and texture.

Obviously, contrast also refers to colour and how drab life would be without it. But never confuse contrast with discord of any kind. Two synonyms of this word are strife and harshness, neither of which has any place in the flower arranger's dictionary.

In fact, contrast presents a challenge: it is relatively quick and easy to make a small design with one kind of flower in one colour. But as soon as you begin to add other subjects, then you need to evaluate how much, where and, indeed, if. Decisions have to be made all along the line, entirely on your own for, as with colour, no two people will agree one hundred per cent on any given balance of contrast.

LEFT *This is a monochromatic colour scheme in tints, tones and shades of red. Materials include bottle, stock and modelling clay; pink drape; bottle filled with water tinted red. Flora are copper beech, spray carnations, roses, heuchera, escalonia.*

ABOVE *An all-yellow design is given a strong focal point by inserting a few stems of magenta stock into the centre.*

USEFUL FLOWERS FOR ARRANGING

Spring flowers offer the flower arranger a fantastic range of materials, including colour, form and size – a complete palette from which to choose, mix, match and harmonize.

Spring Flowers

In the Northern Hemisphere, the daffodil is the true spring flower and, even though it can often be bought in flower shops well before Christmas, it is still thought of as the signal that winter is almost past. For many years now daffodils have been sold in fairly tight bud as it was found that the flowers suffered less damage if they were harvested and packed at what is called the 'gooseneck' stage. That is, when the flower has turned downwards ready to show

EARLY SPRING

Daffodils, tulips, anemones and hyacinths. Irises come into the shops now, and although a bit more expensive than the other flowers mentioned, they do seem to last longer at this time of year.

MID-SPRING

Tulips, daffodils, irises, narcissi, long-stemmed French anemones, hyacinths, ranunculus and wallflowers (Cheiranthus species, or gillyflower). Also small bulb flowers are occasionally found, depending on the florist that you use.

LATE SPRING

Daffodils are mainly finished, although I have on occasion bought them in the very early spring. Late tulips are still available, and irises are normally as inexpensive and abundant as they are likely to get.

Camellia japonica *became very popular during the Victorian era. The flowers, which are often semi-double, can be pink, white or red; some varieties are striped or mottled. They prefer shaded areas and soil that has plenty of organic matter.*

colour. To cut them before this stage would be too early and the flowers would not develop to their true size and beauty. Tulips, irises and freesias are also commercially packed in bud, as are many hybrid lilies such as the lovely orange Enchantment, clear yellow Destiny or Connecticut King and the beautiful white variety called Juliana. They obviously travel better in bud and will open gradually to give a succession of flowers all on one stem.

If spring flowers are bought fresh from the florist, their conditioning is very simple. As a general rule, all bulb-grown flowers should be stood in only a small amount of water, about 3–4in (8–10cm), to which flower food has been added. It is not always essential to cut the stems of daffodils, tulips or freesias, as they drink easily, and cutting the stem-end would cause the flower to open more readily.

Anemones, also, prefer a shallow amount of water. Most lilies usually have rather woody stems and these should be cut with a sharp knife before being conditioned in shallow flower-food solution. It is advisable to leave your spring flowers for an hour or so in as cool and dark a place as possible so that the stems can take up plenty of water. This will reward you with healthy-looking blooms and several days' longer vase life.

Tulips like to curve towards the light and frequently this adds movement and interest to a design. But if you want your tulips to stand upright, you may have to insert wires into their stems, taking care not to puncture them. Insert the wire upwards until you feel it come into contact with the seedbox inside the tulip. The flower should then remain nice and stiff. Polyanthus, like daffodils and tulips, look their best when arranged comparatively informally. Unlike most other flowers, they seem to prefer to be packed tightly into the vase. This does not sound like flower arranging at all, but usually when they are used singly, they hang their heads no matter how well they have been conditioned. Garden-grown lilies-of-the-valley are very similar in this respect, preferring to be 'arranged' in a close-packed, hand-made bouquet and set into a narrow vase, rather than each stem being put in separately. All flowers enjoy an overhead spray with clear water after being arranged.

Try, whenever possible, to use each flower's natural foliage for arranging. Tulips have plenty of leaves, as do irises and violets. Polyanthus leaves will droop unless they have been submerged in water for at least an hour, but after a good 'drowning' they will last just as long as the flowers.

The many beautiful spring-flowering garden shrubs are excellent for large arrangements. Sprays of bright yellow forsythia, delicate prunus, very early-flowering winter jasmine and 'fingers' of witch-hazel on bare branches will all mix happily, either with bulb-grown flowers or by themselves.

Tolmiea

Lily

Lilac

Alyssum

Nettle (yellow archangel)

Iris

Anemone

Gerbera

BELOW *The wild daffodil or Lent lily* (Narcissus pseudonarcissus) *is one of more than 8,000 varieties of narcissus and is common in drifts amongst grass or in borders.*

Ixia

Carnation

Cowslip

Freesia

Liatris

Lily-of-the-valley

Anthurium

Summer Flowers

Summer brings an abundance of flowers in many varieties of size, shape and colour. Even if you do not have a garden, you can still plant flowers in window boxes, planters, and hanging baskets. As long as the plants have light, regular watering and feeding, they will reward you with as many blooms as they would in the garden.

It is a joy to be able to pick flowers from the garden, cutting them precisely when you want them and standing them in water before arranging them.

If there is a quantity of one sort, you can make a one-type flower arrangement with emphasis on line and shape.

EARLY SUMMER

Sees the start of the warm-weather flowers, with cornflowers, lilies, sweet williams, carnations, larkspur, antirrhinum (snap-dragon) and roses available at reasonable prices.

MIDSUMMER

This time of year brings scabious, gypsophila (baby's breath), alstroemeria, cornflowers, larkspur, roses, spray carnations and carnations. Sweet peas and lilies are usually at their peak at this time of year. Bunches of statice and helichrysum start to appear in the shops; since these can be dried for winter use, you can use them fresh and perhaps dry half of your bunch for winter use.

LATE SUMMER

Scabious are usually over, but most of the other flowers that were available in midsummer are still plentiful, in addition to marigolds, gladioli and dahlias, which start to appear at this time. Asters are available toward the end of the period. Other flowers such as statice and rhodanthe are sometimes available in limited quantity.

And if there are still too many, then they can be dried gradually for the winter months. If there are many different types of flowers all blooming at once you can mix them together, making sure that the smaller flowers are not overpowered by the larger varieties.

Before cutting the flowers, do remember to have a container with about 5in (13cm) of water and flower food ready to put them in. In this way your flowers will last as long as possible. Summer storms can spoil lovely blooms, so sometimes it is better to bring them indoors rather than leave them to be beaten down by wind and rain.

A basket is an appropriate container for a mixture of summer flowers and foliage, different colours and textures, shapes and sizes, will all blend happily together. Be sure to condition all the material well. Poppies, for instance, will survive only a day or two, but are lovely while they last. Immediately after cutting, stand them in about 2in (5cm) of almost boiling water and leave them until the water cools. Then add them to the arrangement.

Roses and their sweet-cented perfume epitomize summer. One of the happiest sensations for the keen gardener and flower arranger is picking the first bud of the season and watching it expand.

In his *Herball* of 1599, Gerard observes that although the rose is 'a shrub full of prickles', yet it should not be planted amongst other shrubs but given a place of honour amongst the 'most glorious flowers of the world'.

The rose is not only one of the most beautiful of shrubs, offering a great variety of shapes, colours and sizes, it is also extremely hardy. It will bloom in what seem quite inappropriate situations where lesser flowers might just die.

From the arranger's point of view, roses are particularly adaptable, they are ideal for gifts, bridal bouquets, table centrepieces – and one perfect bud on a gift-wrapped parcel makes it look twice as special. Roses are also suitable for funeral and sympathy tributes and for buttonholes; while for a dedicated flower arranger, the gift of a new variety for the garden makes a wonderful present, for it is hoped that no garden is so well stocked that there is no space for another variety of rose.

Roses also look good in almost any kind of container.

LEFT *The foxglove* (Digitalis purpurea) *is a classic cottage garden species with useful medicinal properties. A biennial, it is common in borders especially in shady areas.*

Philadelphus

Delphinium

Sunflower

Antirrhinum

Potato flower

Molucella

The bird of paradise (Strelitzia reginae) is a favourite with Australian gardeners although it is a native of South Africa. An evergreen, it is much used in flower arrangements.

Alchemilla

Lupin

Hypericum

Geranium

Rose

Pansy

Larkspur

Allium

Geranium

Antirrhinum

Dianthus

Rhododendron

Sweet pea

Chrysanthemum

Eremurus

A colourful display of red, orange and yellow roses – with a light edging of pale green fern. Notice the contrasting curve of the container.

Hydrangea

Sweet William

Loosestrife

Phlox

Marigold

Clarkia

Clematis

Candytuft

Cymbidium

Geranium

Single poppy

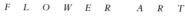

Autumn and Winter Flowers

Autumn is the season of mists and mellow fruitfulness, with string beans, blackberries and grapes – hanging thick and black patiently waiting to be made into wine – bright orange Chinese lanterns (physalis), multicoloured statice and honesty 'moons', and the pinky-mauve fingers of autumn crocus (colchicum).

The whole dahlia family offers a fantastic choice of colour, shape and size. It includes huge decorative blooms the size of a dinner plate, the medium-sized pompom variety, the spiky cactus type and the really tiny button dahlias which, incidentally, make perfect buttonholes, while the creamy white variety make ideal yet simple bridal bouquets. Even though dahlias, and many other flowers, are circular, a line effect can be achieved by carefully grading the colour and size. Try to use each flower the way it faces naturally and profit by any curving stem that will emphasize your line. Remove most of the foliage, for however much one enjoys leaves, dahlia foliage is not always very decorative and it does need a lot of water. Side buds should be cut off and inserted on their own stems.

The Christmas rose (Helleborus niger) *thrives in some gardens but not in others: it prefers partial shade and a soil that is rich and moist. Flowers cut in bud !ast quite well in water.*

EARLY AUTUMN

Dahlias are in full swing, with a great variety of form and colour, and chrysanthemums are appearing cheaply again; gladioli are still available but starting to go up in price. Asters are a good buy.

MID-AUTUMN

Chrysanthemums start to come in bunches and are very good buys at this time of year. Spray chrysanthemums are good value as well. Look out for Chinese lanterns for drying. Other flowers are available but starting to get more expensive. The amaryllis-like nerine and Schizostylis coccinea, or Kaffir lily, are reasonably priced.

LATE AUTUMN

It's still chrysanthemum season, but luckily they come in a wide variety of colours and forms, so there is no danger of getting bored with them. Try the rayonnante or anemone-flowered type for a change. Anemones are also available.

EARLY WINTER

Apart from our friend the chrysanthemum and possibly small flowers like anemones, this is the most expensive time of year for flowers; but take heart, for if you buy a small bunch of freesias or some of the first daffodils, they will last much longer at this time of year. Sugar-pine foliage is also a good buy, and can form an impressive background for north-temperate holiday arrangements. Holly and mistletoe are available, but the quality does vary according to the weather conditions prevalent during the year.

MIDWINTER

Chrysanthemums, snowdrops, anemones, mimosa, violets and tulips.

LATE WINTER

Same as mid-winter, with some daffodils starting to be reasonable.

Erigeron

Physalis

Gladiolus

Sedum

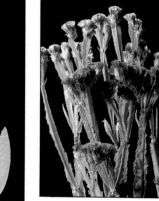

Statice

Snowdrops (Galanthus nivalis) *like
positions under deciduous trees where
winter sun can penetrate. They grow
anywhere, provided that the soil does
not dry out. The flowers are faintly
scented of honey.*

FLOWER ARRANGING CLUBS AND SHOWS

The inexperienced flower arranger should try to join a flower club or horticultural society, preferably one where instruction in the art of flower arrangement is given. This will help to protect your own work, for others can point out details you might have missed, or make otherwise helpful suggestions. A club gives you the opportunity to discuss flower arranging with fellow enthusiasts; you can swap plants and cuttings, and increase your knowledge of horticultural subjects. In Britain there are many flower clubs throughout the length and breadth of the land, and many of these are affiliated with the National Association of Flower Arranging Societies (generally known as N.A.F.A.S.), whose rules and standard definitions are accepted at the majority of flower shows. Likewise, the United States, Australia, and European countries have myriad flower clubs. Any flower show will have information on clubs and societies in the area, or just call up a public garden and ask someone there to suggest a local group to you.

Flower clubs vary in the way they operate; some hold classes or 'teach-ins'; some engage regular demonstrators to show different aspects of flower arranging. Most hold competitive shows, and run various social functions.

One of the most interesting flower club activities is participating in flower festivals or exhibitions, which are held to raise funds for churches or various charities. Experienced flower arrangers are often enlisted to help organize various aspects of these festivals.

Once you become involved with a flower club you may be asked to help establish a schedule for the club show, a task requiring serious consideration. The standard of the club's arrangers can vary within each club, but most clubs comprise a few very good arrangers, some average arrangers and the rest novices. You should see to it that your schedule caters to all three levels of experience in terms of the themes that will suit the members' respective capabilities.

There is very little point in asking novices for an abstract theme, but they may well be able to cope with 'a basket of garden flowers'. The very good arrangers usually like a challenge, so a more difficult class can be set for them.

Some clubs are fortunate to have members who are very good at the flower crafts, and if your club is such a one, try to include a class featuring a picture, plaque or any kind of flower-craft project.

Most shows in England are now judged by the N.A.F.A.S. Schedule Definitions, which you should read and thoroughly understand. The United States has its own State Garden Clubs, each with its own definitions. However, it is also true that many small horticultural shows including floral art in their schedules have their *own* sets of rules, which may well be different from those of the N.A.F.A.S. or State Garden Clubs. So give the rules careful consideration when your schedule arrives.

Don't leave your planning until the last minute. Make rough sketches of your proposed designs at least two to three weeks before the show. Check local florists to ensure that the flowers you require will be available. Look for suitable containers and bases. Try out the mechanics and staging, using a tape measure to check your height, depth and width against the requirements of the schedule.

Condition all plant material to be used, and groom all leaves so that they have no holes or ragged edges. Make sure you have all the things you require – a check list is a good idea, since it may save you from arriving at the show minus a vital component.

Take a few spare flowers and pieces of foliage in case of accident, and some spare floral foam and/or pinholders. It sometimes helps to tie the material for each arrangement in separate bunches, especially if you are making more than one arrangement. Make sure that any drapes you utilize are ironed and crease-free; put them around a cardboard roll to carry them to the show.

Don't take on more than you can comfortably manage. When you are actually doing your arrangement be self-critical: stand back and look at it; can you see any gaps, are there any mechanics visible, would moving an accessory slightly give a better line? If you can see any of these faults, correct them. Then leave well alone.

Books on period design are of particular value to those who exhibit at shows. You may not be able to procure the exact, authentic materials (for example, old-fashioned roses, although modern roses with an old-fashioned look can often be obtained), but you can usually create the feeling of a certain period by studying the containers and the types of plant material that were used at the time.

LEFT *This is an interpretive design to portray the traditional final night of London's famous Promenade Concerts. The black canes are notched to represent flutes, black and white represent the piano and the orchestra, and the carnation is for the conductor's buttonhole. Party streamers are what the audience throw, and the music is 'Land of Hope and Glory', always sung on the last night.*

Materials: painted tin can with soaked floral foam, large base, party streamer, sheet music. Cane leaves, black-painted trimmed palm leaves, carnations and spray carnations, iris leaves, magnolia leaves.

1 Place the cane and palm leaves at the back and sides. 2 Add one palm leaf to the front. 3 Add buds and spray carnations at the side, bringing the large ones to the centre. 4 Fill in with the iris and magnolia leaves. 5 Add the party streamer to run through the design. 6 Place the design on a base and add the sheet music.

Pressing

EQUIPMENT

One of the great advantages of this craft is that you can start without spending very much money. In fact it may well be that you already have most of what you need at home, and that a variety of everyday household objects will now become the essential tools of your craft. It is a good idea to assemble the following items.

The most important piece of equipment is, of course, something in which to press the flowers. This could be simply a large book, or it might be a flower press specifically designed for the job.

An out-of-date telephone directory is ideal as a pressing book because it has the right sort of absorbent paper. Books with glossy pages are unsuitable as they can encourage mildew. A second advantage of a phone book is that it does not matter if its spine is eventually damaged by the thickness of the layers of flowers. (Naturally it would be unwise to use the family bible or any other treasured volume for this purpose!) Whatever large, expendable book is used, additional weight is necessary for successful pressing. This could be provided in the form of other books or bricks.

Although the phone-book method can be perfectly effective, a press is preferable. This is because it puts the flowers under greater pressure and therefore speeds the drying process. Also, carefully prepared flowers are rather less likely to be disturbed by having the separate layers of blotting paper and corrugated paper placed on them from above, than by the sideways action of closing a book.

Many craft shops and quality toy shops now sell flower presses. These are fine – but avoid making the mistake of buying the smallest ones, which measure about 4in (10cm) square. The disadvantage of these is that, although they are pretty and can be used effectively for small flowers, they have severe limitations if you want to press such essential elements as grasses and long, gracefully curving stems. The ideal size for a press is about 9in (23cm) square. Larger ones can become very heavy and, unless they have some special device for maintaining pressure in the middle, the two pieces of wood which sandwich the pressed material may develop a tendency to bow or warp. The result of this is that the flowers in the middle are under less pressure than those around the edge, and are therefore at risk of shrivelling or becoming mildewed.

BELOW AND BELOW RIGHT Useful tools. *1 A fine soft brush to tease off slightly sticky pressed specimens from their blotting paper beds, to move delicate flowers around during design work, or to brush surplus pollen from flowers such as buttercups. 2 Pencils and pens for a variety of jobs, from indexing storage books to doing decorative line work. 3 Cocktail sticks or toothpicks, for applying tiny amounts of glue to flowers. 4 A ruler – metal if possible – to ensure straight edges. 5 A retractable craft knife for cutting card and mountboard, preferably of the type that has a blade with several snap-off sections, so that the blade is always sharp. 6 Scissors: a large pair for cutting paper, fabric and other material and 7 a smaller pair for use with plant material. 8 A small pair tweezers for picking up delicate plant material or for working with various jewellery-type settings.*

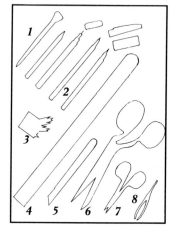

FAR RIGHT TOP A finished press, together with a lightweight travelling press.

FAR RIGHT BOTTOM Some of the many richly coloured velvets which make ideal backgrounds for flower designs.

Making Your Own Press

This is relatively simple and should ensure that you get exactly what you want in size, weight, the number of layers, and so on.

MATERIALS FOR MAKING A PRESS 1 Two pieces of sturdy wood such as plywood, measuring about 9in (23cm) square and ½in (1cm) thick (9-ply is ideal and should not warp). 2 Four 3in (8cm) bolts with wingnuts to fit. 3 Three large sheets of blotting paper. 4 Some stiff corrugated card which can be cut from packing material.

Rub down the surfaces and edges of the plywood with sandpaper. Place the two pieces together, one on top of the other, and drill holes large enough to take your bolts in each of the four corners, about ¾in (2cm) from the edge; fix the bolts into the bottom piece of wood, gluing the heads securely into position. Cut 12 8in (20cm) squares of blotting paper, trimming off triangular pieces at the corners to accommodate the bolts; cut 7 pieces of corrugated card of the same size and shape. Starting and ending with card, interleave two pieces of blotting paper with each layer of card. Place this card and blotting paper 'sandwich' on the wooden base; locate the top piece of wood on the bolts and secure the wingnuts.

You might also find a lightweight travelling press an ideal companion on a country expedition. It can be made on the same principle as the sturdy press, but smaller and lighter.

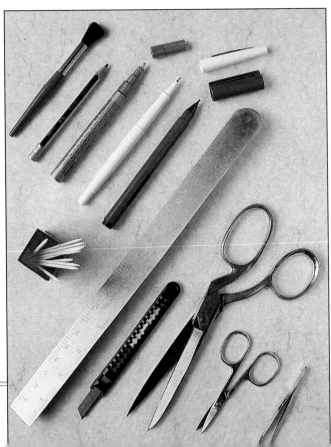

Storage Equipment

You will need to find some means of storing pressed material in good condition until you are ready to use it. This should be easy because, whether or not you have used old telephone directories for pressing, they certainly make excellent means of storage. You may find it useful to keep several of these books, each one reserved for a different type of plant material.

Some people prefer to store each type of flower in an individual bag. This method is fine, if the bags are porous so that the flower can 'breathe'. Plastic bags are not recommended: they could trap any remaining moisture. The ideal bag for the purpose is one which has a paper back for porosity, and a cellophane front for visibility. If bags are to be used, a convenient means must be found of keeping them under some pressure. Inside telephone books perhaps?

Amid the paraphernalia of the flower presser's craft, decorative flowers (including alstroemerias, sweet peas and pansies) await their transformation into decorative design.

ABOVE *A typical pressing book, used here for pressing heather. Additional weight is provided in the form of two bricks.*

Design Materials

ABOVE *The various materials which may be used to protect finished flower designs. 1 Clear varnish 2 Acetate 3 Coating resin 4 Glass 5 Clear self-adhesive covering film.*

When you are ready to begin making designs, you will need a range of materials. Most of these should be as easily available as the equipment described previously. Items required include design backgrounds, such as paper, card or fabric, as well as glues, and some protective coverings.

Paper or card should be of good quality and have an attractive colour and texture. In addition to the materials that can be purchased from art and craft shops, the range of ordinary coloured writing papers now available offers a delightful choice; moreover, plain areas of thin card are often to be found in suitable colours and sizes on attractive packaging material.

It is preferable to use fabric as a background for most flower designs. This is because its range and subtlety of colour and texture is even greater than that now available in paper and card. Patterned and heavily textured fabrics are obviously not suitable for design backgrounds, but almost any fabric that looks good with flowers will do.

Velvet has a rich depth of colour which changes according to the angle at which you look at the design, and becomes lighter in colour where greater pressure is applied (around the edge of a picture, for example, where the veneer pins or locking plate grip most firmly). Satins have a beautiful sheen, and are suitable for use with the most delicate flowers.

Acquiring fabrics should not involve too much expense. It is not necessary, for example, to purchase the most costly dress satins: lining satins can be just as attractive and, although velvet is usually expensive, you require only small pieces and might discover just what you need on the remnant counter. Remember also that either furnishing or dress-making fabric will serve the purpose; any plain-coloured leftovers from other handiwork can be put to good use. Best of all, you might be fortunate enough to acquire one or two out-of-date swatches of plain fabric colour samples, as used in large furnishing fabric departments. You would then have an amazing range of colours from which to choose.

All but the sturdiest fabrics are easier to work with if they are given more body by being backed with a self-adhesive covering (of the sort normally used for such purposes as covering shelves). Any pattern is unimportant, for it will not show.

The most important type of glue required is the one that sticks the flowers to their background. For this purpose, I prefer to use a latex adhesive which can be applied in tiny amounts on the end of a cocktail stick. You may also need other types of glue from time to time, including one for bonding paper and card. This is most conveniently available in the form of a solid adhesive stick.

Once a design has been glued into position . It should be covered in some way that ensures permanent protection for the flowers. A variety of materials may be used for this purpose: clear self-adhesive covering film, varnish, resin, acetate or glass.

BELOW LEFT Two examples of the sort of colourful fabric swatches which you might be lucky enough to acquire from the furnishing fabric departments of large stores.

BELOW Design backgrounds backed with a self-adhesive covering to give them more body. (Apply this backing before cutting the background to size.)

COLLECTING FLOWERS

*I*f you are lucky enough to have somewhere to grow your own flowers, your work may begin long before the collecting stage. There is the delight of choosing the seed packets most likely to produce blooms good for pressing. Then there are the pleasures of planting the seeds, tending the young plants and watching them grow to maturity.

When collecting flowers for pressing, the aim should always be to pick the best specimens in the best conditions. This is relatively easy with flowers picked very near your home since you can choose just when to pick them. Several factors should be taken into account when deciding on the optimum time for picking.

Flowers must be picked at the right stage in their development. This stage is usually reached shortly after they have emerged from the bud, when their colour is at its richest. Occasionally, buds are more useful to the flower-presser than the open form, as in the case of tightly closed dark-orange montbretia buds. Many designs are enhanced by the use of both buds and open specimens of the same flower, so it is often a good idea to press them in both forms. But do not succumb to the temptation of trying to enjoy the beauty of the flowers on the plant for as long as possible, picking them for pressing only just before they fade or drop. This does not give good results.

Foliage also has to be picked at the right stage of development. The very young leaves of eccremocarpus, for example, and those of *Clematis montana* emerge from the press a striking black colour. If picked when too mature, they turn out a much less inspiring flat green. Even grasses should be watched for the right stage – their delicate spikelets should be open, but not so far developed that they are ready to shed their seeds all over your designs.

Pick each species early in its season when the plants are lush and sappy – they will press far more successfully than those which appear later in the season.

Another important factor to consider is the weather. Damp is the flower-presser's main enemy: it encourages mildew. Specimens should therefore be collected on a dry day when any droplets of water from the showers of previous days are likely to have evaporated.

A collection of flowers sealed in an inflated plastic bag in order to maintain their freshness, as it was not possible to press them immediately.

ABOVE Collecting celandines for pressing.

ABOVE Collecting forget-me-nots for pressing.

The time of day is also important: a sunny afternoon is the best time of all. Even a fine morning may be damp with dew and, by early evening, some flowers will have closed for the night.

The final luxury of picking flowers locally is that it is practical to pick a few specimens at a time and to put them straight into the press before there is any possibility that their condition can deteriorate.

When travelling farther afield to collect flowers, it may be more difficult to ensure ideal conditions. However, the guidelines listed above still apply. The major problem is likely to be keeping the flowers fresh. If they have wilted by the time you arrive back home, it will be much more difficult to press them successfully.

Of the two major methods for maintaining freshness, one is to use a travelling press and with it to press the flowers as soon as possible after picking them, preferably in a sheltered spot. When you arrive home, the card and blotting paper 'sandwiches' with the flowers undisturbed inside, can be simply transferred to the main press. (Alternatively, if the travelling press is not likely to be required again for a while, you can put it under an additional weight and leave it exactly as it is.)

The second method of maintaining freshness is to carry around several airtight plastic bags. Collect the specimens directly into the bags – not too many in each or they may crush each other. When you have finished collecting, blow air into each bag, as if you were blowing up a balloon, and secure the top with a flexible tie. This air cushion serves to prevent the flowers from becoming crushed, over-heated or dried out. They should then arrive home – even many hours later – as fresh as when they were picked.

Remember to pick only perfect specimens. Pressing cannot improve a substandard bloom – and your designs can only be as beautiful as the individual flowers that make them up.

ABOVE *Pressed specimens of flowers that need some preparation before successful pressing can take place. 1 Love-in-a-mist and 2 London pride should both have their projecting seedboxes removed. The seed box behind the dog rose 3 also needs removing. The multi-flowered heads of elderflowers 4 must be separated into small sprays while hydrangea florets 5 must be pressed individually.*

TECHNIQUES IN PRESSING

The flowers and foliage collected will be of many different types, shapes and sizes. It may not always be possible to put them straight into a press without some form of preparation. Various techniques are involved.

The simplest flowers to press are those that are flat or like a shallow dish in shape. Buttercups are a good example of this type and can be persuaded easily into a new two-dimensional state.

Remove any part of a flower which might impair the appearance of the whole after it has been pressed. When flowers are to be pressed in the open form, for example, it is wise to remove stems from all but the sturdiest, in order to prevent them from bruising or deforming the petals under which they lie. For the same reason, certain parts of flowers – like the green calyx which sheathes the back of a primrose – are best removed.

Another reason for removing flower parts is to facilitate the transformation into the two-dimensional. Both love-in-a-mist (devil-in-the-bush) and London pride press well, once the seedboxes which project in front have been removed. The same can be said of the single dog rose after the careful removal of the seedbox from behind the flower.

TOP *It is a good idea to remove both the stem and the calyx of a primrose before pressing. The calyx might otherwise bruise the delicate petal under which it lies.*

ABOVE *Forget-me-not stems should be prepared for pressing by removing some of the individual flowers to prevent overcrowding. The spiral of buds at the top of the stem may also be pressed separately.*

LEFT *The three-dimensional daffodil can be sliced in two and pressed in profile.*

ABOVE. *All but the smallest rosebuds must be separated into individual petals before pressing. Press the green sepals for the later reconstruction of rosebuds.*

Multiple flowers may be prepared in a variety of ways. Some, like elderflowers, can be pressed effectively either as a whole or in small sprays, as long as the groups of florets are spread out as much as possible when being placed in the press. The flower-packed heads of a hydrangea, usually bearing well over 100 florets, may seem a daunting prospect until it is realized that each one can be removed and pressed separately, like any flat flower, One of the multiple flowers which best repays preparatory work is the forget-me-not. If the stems are pressed unprepared, the many flowers – which had plenty of space in their three-dimensional growing state – will be overcrowded and develop unattractive marks wherever they have overlapped the stem or each other. If you thin them out, however, you will be doubly rewarded with graceful curving stems of undamaged flowers, and by the individual 'thinnings' which press into tiny circles of sky-blue perfection.

So far, I have considered only flowers that can be converted relatively easily to the two-dimensional. But what of truly three-dimensional flowers like daffodils, roses and carnations? It could be argued that these are best left alone by the flower-presser.

Daffodils can be pressed effectively by removing the seedbox and slicing through the trumpet, after which it is possible to press the two resulting 'profiles'. The same slicing technique can be used on very small rosebuds: larger ones, however, must be treated differently: remove the green sepals for separate pressing, and then carefully peel the delicate satin-smooth petals from the bud so that each one can be pressed individually. (When making rose designs later on, you can reconstruct 'buds' by building up layers of individual petals and using the centres of rock roses as false, but fairly true-to-life, middles.)

Carnations can be treated by the same 'separate petal' procedure. Their pressed petals make realistic 'buds' when used in combination with sections of the green sheath-like calyx.

It is always sensible to place only flowers of the same thickness in any one of the layer of the press. This eliminates the risk of putting the flatter ones under insufficient pressure, which could cause shrivelling or encourage mildew. But what if a single flower is itself of uneven thickness? This can sometimes be a problem. One occasionally sees daisies for example whose petals have become spiky because they have not been as heavily pressed as the middles. In the case of such small flowers this problem can usually be overcome by giving the yellow middles an extra firm squeeze before pressing. The solution is not so simple with the bigger daisies, or with other large daisy-type flowers you may want to press. These flowers have middles which are so significantly bulkier than their surrounding petals that it would be impossible to apply even pressure to the whole flower without the use of a 'collar'. This is a series of newspaper or blotting paper circles with the centres cut out to accommodate the thick middle; the correct number of layers of paper can be placed underneath the petals to even up the thickness.

As you gain experience you will develop all sorts of personal techniques for preparing particular flowers and other types of plant material. You may, for example, find it helpful to use a rolling pin to 'pre-press' a particularly thick stem of, say, *Clematis montana*. Alternatively, you may decide to slice it in two before pressing. You will also discover the exceptions to the 'rules' – particularly, perhaps, to the one which decrees that all plant material should be placed in the press as quickly as possible. Moss, for instance, almost invariably comes from a damp habitat and is therefore best left in a warm room for a few hours before pressing.

One final general point about preparation: although you are not necessarily considering the finer details of design at this stage, it is nevertheless helpful to keep the likely eventual designs in mind when you are arranging material in the press. Once the specimens are dried, they are more or less fixed in shape.

ABOVE A single daisy-type chrysanthemum being pressed by the 'collar' method.

ABOVE Clumps of moss should be allowed to dry out in a warm room for several hours before being separated into small pieces for pressing.

The Pressing Process: Hazards

The aim of this stage is to dry and flatten the flowers in such a way as to ensure that they come out of the press as bright and as beautiful as when they went in. There are various hazards from which they must now be protected. The three major ones are undue disturbance, mildew and incorrect pressure.

Once they have been prepared for pressing, flowers should not be disturbed any more than is absolutely necessary. This means that when the press is being filled, its layers of card and blotting paper must be carefully placed one on top of the other, so that the flowers do not move from the position in which you have set them, and none of the leaves or petals is accidentally folded over. Similar precautions should be taken when closing a pressing book: its pages should be gently rolled closed over the precious contents. You should, particularly in the early days, resist the temptation to 'see how they are getting on'. Partly pressed material is very limp and, once misshapen, is difficult to reshape correctly.

Mildew is the most serious risk at the pressing stage. It can be heartbreaking to open the press after several weeks and find everything inside covered with a damp grey mould. This should not happen if the necessary precautions are taken.

Make sure that flowers are under sufficient pressure. Pressing-books must be adequately weighted, and the wing-nuts of presses must be checked every day or two during the first week. This is because as the material in a press dries out, it becomes less bulky so that the nuts need tightening to maintain the pressure.

Keep your presses in a dry, airy place.

To avoid the spread of any mildew if it does occur, make sure that there is plenty of space between the flowers on

ABOVE *A celandine with a missing petal being prepared with a good petal from another blemished specimen.*

each layer, and that the layers themselves are well separated by corrugated card or several intervening pages.

Do not add any new, mosisture-laden material to a press or book already containing drying flowers.

In spite of my advice not to disturb the flowers unnecessarily, it is nevertheless sensible to inspect a few of them after a week or so to check for damp or mildew. If any is found, a more thorough check is indicated, during which you should throw away any even slightly mildewed specimens, and change damp blotting paper or pressing books.

The pressing process for subjects particularly prone to mildew, such as roses and carnations, may be best *startea* in any particularly warm dry place or airing-cupboard. But I would not recommend this for all flowers, or for any flowers for more than a few days. They can become dry and brittle if left too long.

Just as too little pressure can put flowers at risk, so over-pressing can also present a problem. It usually occurs only when a press containing layers of corrugated card is used. Such card is normally invaluable because its corrugations aid ventilation and help to prevent the spread of damp. Also its flexible thickness does much to maintain an even pressure on bulky subjects. If precautions are not taken, however, it can cause imperfections on delicate petals. Primroses, for example, pressed between single sheets of blotting paper sandwiched between this card, could emerge from the press with corrugations imprinted on their petals. You may feel happier using the book method for these tender specimens, but you can still use the press if you insert additional layers of blotting paper, or if perhaps you replace the card altogether with several thicknesses of newspaper.

A final note on pressing: it is worth mentioning that both blotting paper and pressing-books can be re-used indefinitely, if kept perfectly dry and free from mildew.

ABOVE *Some specimens, like the individual flowers of forget-me-nots, have a tendency to stick to blotting paper. They can be teased off with a small, soft brush.*

RIGHT *When using a pressing book, avoid disturbing or damaging specimens by gently rolling closed the pages.*

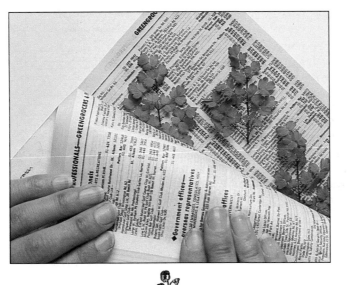

Pressing: Duration

Traditionally, the pressing process takes about six weeks –
a slightly shorter time for small, dry specimens, and a little
longer for those that are larger or more moisture-laden. A
simple test of whether a flower is ready for use is to select a
specimen still on its stem, and hold it up by the base of the
stem. If it stands upright, it is ready; if it flops, it should be
returned to the press for a little while longer.

At the height of summer, when flowers are at their most
abundant, you may find you need a press for new material
before its original contents have been in for long enough. It
is reasonable, in such circumstances, to transfer the flowers
carefully to well-weighted storage books at any time after
the first ten days. If you do this, remember to label them
clearly with the pressing date and not to use them in designs
until the full six-week period is complete.

Other ways of shortening the time in the press involve
the use of modern appliances. The aim of pressing flowers
is to dry and flatten them so you might be forgiven for
thinking that you could do this most efficiently with a
domestic iron! In fact, if plant material is ever needed
urgently (or an otherwise good flower has a creased petal),
it is possible, with the iron on a low-heat setting, to press
sturdy flowers or leaves between sheets of blotting paper.
This process should be followed by a few days under
pressure in a warm, dry place.

Now comes the pleasure of looking through the wealth
of lovely pressed material from which you will soon be
creating designs. If all has gone well, you will have many
perfect two-dimensional representations of the original
specimens in a variety of rich colours. Larkspur duplicate
the shades of the growing flowers; the little annual phlox
(Pride of Texas) undergo subtle colour changes; the
young leaves of eccremocarpus show an even more
dramatic change.

It is sensible to discard any specimens that come out of
the press discoloured or faded, damaged or distorted. There
will always be a small proportion of these, which would
spoil your designs if used. (Do not, however, be too quick
to throw away flowers that are only slightly damaged, for
it may be possible to amalgamate two blemished blooms
into one perfect specimen.)

It is worth mentioning here that although most flowers
obligingly slide straight off their pressing backgrounds
into their new storage accommodation, others need a little
gentle persuasion before they will move. The tiny individual
forget-me-nots, for example, have a tendency to stick to
blotting paper, and each one needs to be patiently teased
off with the soft tip of a fine brush. Fingernails or even
tweezers may cause damage.

ABOVE *A pressed daisy standing upright. It is now completely dry and ready for use.*

RIGHT *A collection of specimens just removed from the press on their blotting paper sheets.*

BELOW *Pressed specimens may be stored in books or cellophane-fronted bags. It is a good idea to label and index books, with dates, so that flowers are disturbed no more than is actually necessary.*

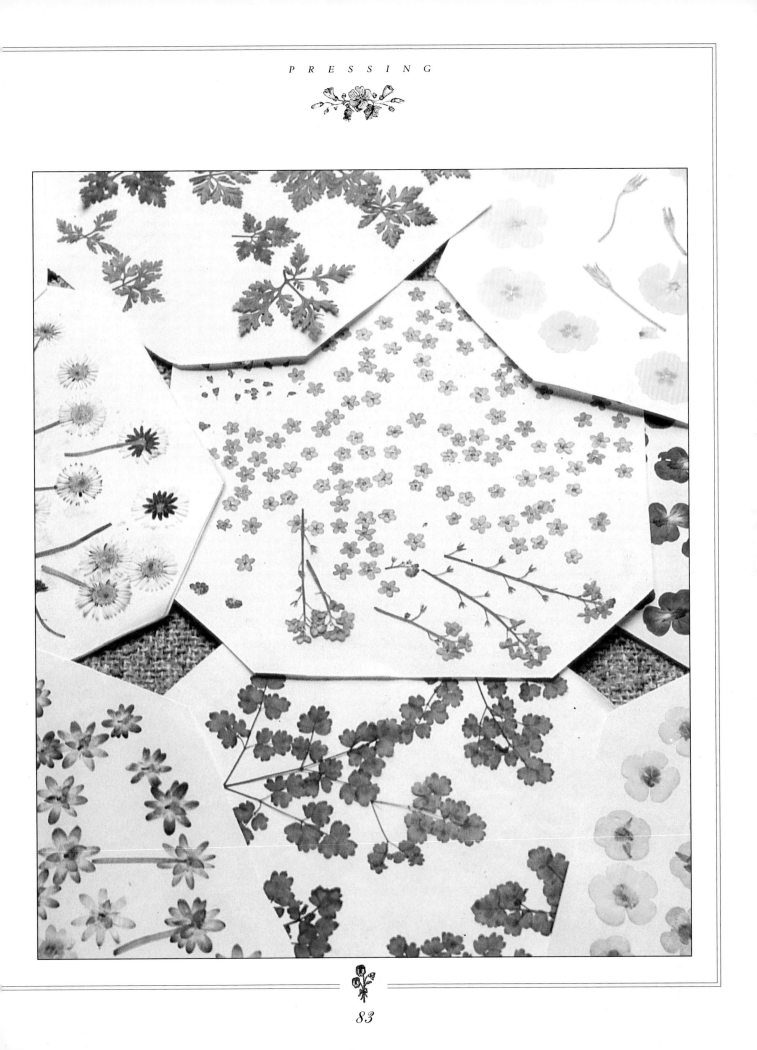

Storage

Once flowers have been pressed, they must remain perm-anently under some form of pressure, whether in storage or in their final settings. Only in this way will they remain in good condition; any exposure to air will put them at risk of reabsorbing moisture.

All pressed specimens are stored in a series of old telephone directories. These are excellent for the purpose because they are freely available, heavy enough to keep the flowers in good shape, and large enough not to overcrowd the specimens. Also, their absorbent pages deal with any poss-ible traces of remaining moisture. Another possibility is to store each type of flower in individual cellophane-fronted, paper-backed bags as described on page 72. Storage books and bags should, like presses, be kept in a dry, airy place and, if piled one on top of another, should be occasionally rearranged so that they are evenly ventilated.

Each type of flower should have its its own bag or section of book, and all the pressed material should be arranged in a logical and easy-to-find order. This is because the 'do-

Unprotected bookmarks. These simple and attractive designs were made with astrantia, buttercups and pansies each of which was carefully stuck down with several tiny areas of glue.

not-disturb-unnecessarily' rule remains as relevant as ever, and repeated searches through randomly-stored flowers for a particular specimen greatly increase the risk of damage.

It is best to keep separate books for miniature flowers, larger flowers, leaves, grasses, and so forth, and within each book the specimens can be arranged in the order in which they appear during the year. As a consequence of this, you will know that early flowers are usually to be found somewhere among the Collinses, while the mid-summer blooms live with the Joneses, and the autumn species with the Wilsons! This information is a little too vague, however, so at the beginning of each book keep a list of page numbers detailing exactly which flowers appear where. As an alternative to such a list, labels identifying flowers can be attached to the relevant pages or bags. These precautions should ensure that you can always find a particular flower quickly and easily, and with the minimum of disturbance to the rest.

Great care is needed when removing specimens from bags and when replacing them if they are surplus to requirements. Also, when turning the pages of storage books you should try to make sure that the contents do not slip towards the spine. If everything collects in this area, the book becomes misshapen – and so do the flowers.

These unprotected greetings cards are made in a similar way to the bookmarks. The pictures include saxifrage, buttercups and astrantia. Note how they can be made even more charming by the addition of a small design inside the card which reflects the main design.

Handling Pressed Flowers

You will be able to remove the sturdiest flowers from their storage books, and move them around on the design background, simply by using your fingers. When dealing with more delicate specimens, however, it may be helpful to use small tweezers to pick them up, and the tip of a fine brush to move them around on the design.

The method many people prefer for the most delicate flowers of all is to moisten the tip of your forefinger very slightly, by touching it just inside your lip. Apply gentle pressure to the flower to be picked up, which then usually sticks to your finger sufficiently well to allow you to transfer it to its new position. The great advantage of this technique is that you do not risk damaging your most fragile specimens by trying to get either fingers or tweezers underneath the petals.

Sticking Down

Once a design is in its setting, the glass – or whatever is used to protect your work – should be holding it so firmly in place, that nothing could possibly move. It is however, so difficult to get an 'unstuck' design into its setting without any of its components moving out of position, that it is almost essential to glue down every single piece.

This does not mean that the whole area of each flower has to be firmly stuck to its background. The smallest possible amount of adhesive should be applied, on the end

BELOW When sticking down a design, use a cocktail stick to apply a tiny spot of latex adhesive to the base of the thickest part of each flower.

BELOW Sticking down overlapping flowers.

ABOVE Snowdrops arranged with the attractive, white-lined spikes of a crocus plant.

BELOW Cowslips whose yellow flowers have turned green

ABOVE The best way of handling a delicate specimen is to apply gentle pressure to it with a slightly moist fingertip. The flower should then stick to your finger for long enough to enable you to move it into the desired position.

of a cocktail stick, to the back of the thickest part of each flower or leaf. Stems should have tiny spots of glue dotted along their length; fine materials like grasses and tendrils need stroking in only one or two places with a lightly glued stick.

You will soon find out if you are using too much glue, because it will show through delicate petals. Worse still, it may squeeze out from underneath and mark the background. If this happens with a latex adhesive, it is often possible to 'roll off' the offending glue by rubbing the marked area with a clean finger.

When you become experienced and are sure of the effect you are trying to create, you may choose to stick down each part of the design as you go along. If you are less experienced, or experimenting with new ideas, it is probably better to lay out the whole design before you stick any of it. Then, taking care not to disturb the surrounding flowers and leaves more than necessary, you can pick up each one separately and gently glue it into position. Where flowers overlap, you must, of course, stick down the underneath ones first.

1

6

3

Retaining Colour

2

5

Colour is not everything. The beauty of a pressed-flower design resides in far more than this, and wonderful effects can be achieved by using the subtlest and most muted of colours. The fact remains, however, that it is lovely to see flower pictures that capture the original brightness of nature. The question most frequently asked by people looking at pressed flowers is, 'How do you keep the colours so bright?' There is no 'magic' involved; if you press the right flowers and use the techniques outlined you have every chance of success.

Your responsibility for helping to retain colours does not end at the point where the flowers are safely in their settings. The position in which they are then displayed is important. No pressed-flower design should be constantly exposed to direct sunlight (so do not stand paperweights on sunny windowsills). Remember also that moisture can continue to be a problem so a room like a damp conservatory could be a disastrous place to hang a flower picture.

There is, of course, one means by which it is possible to make certain that flowers retain their colour. This is the technique, recommended by several books on the subject, of colouring flowers permanently with poster paints. Decide for yourself on this matter. To some, the hard, artificial colours of paint fail to blend with the subtler natural shades of flowers. If a flower is going to lose colour to the point at which it will no longer be attractive, perhaps it would be better not to use it at all.

When dealing with the fine translucent petals of such flowers as the primrose, putting one, or even two, additional flowers on top of the original one will intensify its colour. A daisy with a bright yellow middle but thin petals can be superimposed on one with a discoloured middle but beautiful pink-edged petals. Similar 'tricks' can be employed with foliage. Except when making 'botanical pictures', you could substitute leaves which are more attractive or keep colour

THIS PAGE Colour testers and the lessons to be learnt from them. *1 Forget-me-nots, spiraea (both white and pink), saxifrage and the veined petals of the ballerina geranium all keep their colour well. The alpine phlox and the purple lobelia (as opposed to the blue one) do not. 2 Montbretia buds and hypericum keep colour beautifully. 3 All the flowers in this frame (blue lobelia, heuchera, lady's mantle, astrantia and the heather florets) have proved reliable. 4 This frame shows that the larkspur and delphinium (right) are better colour-keepers than the love-in-a-mist (left). 5 The hardy fuschsia is seen to keep colour reliably. 6 The 'everlasting' helipterum and anaphalis included here are still bright as is the darker of the rock roses.*

It is apparent from these colour testers that, while foliage which presses black or silver maintains its original colour, almost all green foliage fades.

4

RIGHT AND ABOVE Ways of
improving colour naturally. *Three
primroses have been superimposed here
to intensify their delicate colour, and
interest is added to the large daisy by
the superimposition of a slightly
smaller pink-edged specimen.*

better than a particular flower's own leaves. When working
with snowdrops, for example, you can use the similar but
prettier white-lined crocus spikes.

The whole subject of colour retention in pressed flowers
is fascinating, and the only way to study it satisfactorily is
to observe the various changes which take place over the
years. This requires patience, of course, but you will, in
time, be rewarded by knowing which flowers are going to
retain their colours most reliably.

A series of 'colour testers', comprising a wide variety of
flowers mounted in frames, will show you what the passing
years do to them. The flowers and foliage fall into three
categories: those that keep their colour well; those that pale
down but are still beautiful enough to be worth using against
the right background; and those that, regretfully, are not
worth pressing again. One of the greatest surprises with
respect to a bizarre colour-change was the once limpid
yellow cowslips: they are now bright green!

AESTHETIC PRINCIPLES

O nce you have a collection of good pressed mat-erial, you are ready to proceed with confidence to the design stage. Sadly, however, this is just the point at which many people come to a standstill. The design section of books on flower-pressing with their references to 'contour', 'balance', 'harmony' and other technicalities can be somewhat daunting to a beginner. Therefore what follows is an absolutely practical approach. Of course, this is not the only way to begin, but it should help you to build up confidence as you progress. Try working through the following steps, using your own choice of flowers, introducing variations whenever you wish, and abandoning my suggestions altogether at the point at which you find your own style.

Start Small, Start Simple

Choose a small setting and be prepared, at this stage, to rely entirely on the beauty of one individual flower to create the design. Choose your flower with care, for you will not get away with such complete simplicity unless it is a perfect specimen, and unless it is sufficiently intricate or visually interesting to satisfy the eye. Background colour and texture are all important, the use of fabric is recommended for the additional interest it can provide. (Try placing your flower

THIS PAGE Start small, start simple. *Four 'designs' each relying on the beauty of the individual flowers to create the finished effect. 1 Love-in-a-mist 2 Burnet Saxifrage 3 Astrantia 4 Wild Carrot.*

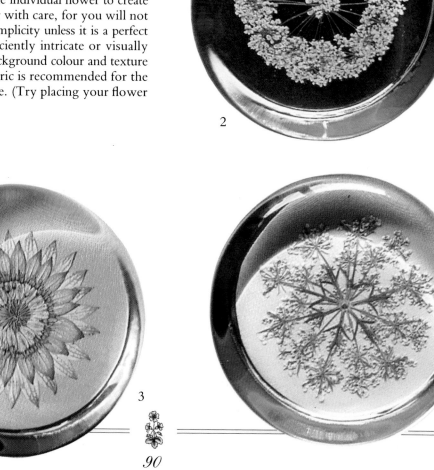

1

2

3

4

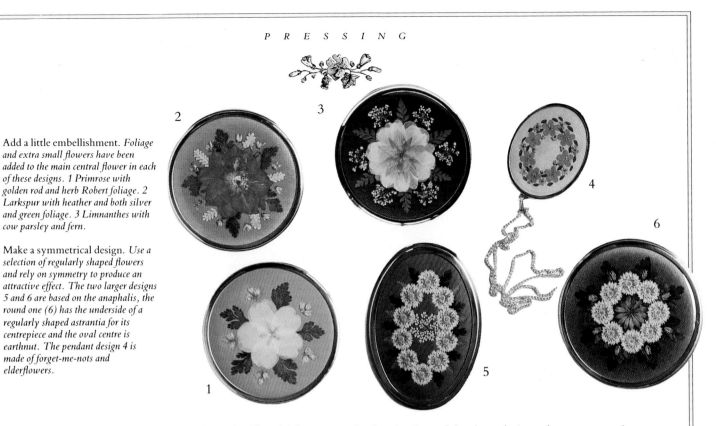

Add a little embellishment. *Foliage and extra small flowers have been added to the main central flower in each of these designs. 1 Primrose with golden rod and herb Robert foliage. 2 Larkspur with heather and both silver and green foliage. 3 Limnanthes with cow parsley and fern.*

Make a symmetrical design. *Use a selection of regularly shaped flowers and rely on symmetry to produce an attractive effect. The two larger designs 5 and 6 are based on the anaphalis, the round one (6) has the underside of a regularly shaped astrantia for its centrepiece and the oval centre is earthnut. The pendant design 4 is made of forget-me-nots and elderflowers.*

on a variety of different backgrounds to decide which one enhances it most.) Finally, try to ensure that your work is technically perfect, for a badly positioned flower, a roughly cut-out piece of fabric, or a single spot of unwanted glue can mar simple designs.

An ideal flower for this purpose is the astrantia. With its tiny flowers and surrounding pointed bracts, it needs no further embellishment.

Another particularly suitable candidate for the simple approach is love-in-a-mist (devil-in-a-bush), with its dark green central stamens and fine misty-green foliage that surrounds the flower. A little judicious rearrangement might be necessary if this foliage is not evenly spread, but basically it is still the simple beauty of the flower which does the design work.

The lacy flower-heads of the Umbellifers are also sufficiently intricate to stand alone.

You should as you gain experience succeed in making larger and more elaborate pressed flower pictures. But for sheer simple beauty, you may never make anything to surpass these small, one-flower 'designs' in which the patience, care and technique are yours but the art is all nature's.

Add a Little Embellishment

Begin again with a single central flower, but this time, use a slightly larger setting and add some pieces of foliage, radiating from the centre. Then introduce some other tiny flowers in colours that blend both with the central specimen and with the background.

In the simplest of the three designs shown, two primroses have been placed one on top of the other to intensify their pale colour. The shape of the petals has been allowed to suggest the position of the five pieces of herb Robert leaf, and three single florets of golden rod, whose deeper colour blends with the pale primroses, have been arranged in each of the spaces thus created.

The *Limnanthes* design on the darker green also uses two superimposed central flowers, this time with the pale green leaves of a delicate fern in the shape of a six-pointed star, and the heads of cow parsley, making a dainty space-filler.

The design using the central larkspur is the most complex, using two contrasting types of foliage, with the pink heather florets as space-fillers.

Make a Symmetrical Design

Having made some semi-regular designs based on a single central flower, you will want to progress to more complex work. One way to introduce this is to try something completely symmetrical. Pressed-flower pictures should always be balanced and in proportion, but they certainly need not be symmetrical. Indeed, it would be very limiting to make only regular designs. These can, however, be beautiful, and the reason for considering them here is that it is not difficult, even for a beginner, to think out a symmetrical design that works well. This does not mean that they are easy to make from a technical point of view. They demand quite as much care and patience in choosing and positioning flowers and foliage, which must be carefully selected for their regularity of both size and shape.

Try working with the beautifully regular anaphalis (pearly everlasting), together with the leaves of herb Robert. If these are unobtainable, you may be able to find enough regular specimens of the equally attractive common daisy. Among the smaller flowers that work well in symmetrical designs are forget-me-nots, London pride, spiraea and elder-flower. You will see from the examples that this sort of design succeeds equally well in round or oval settings. It could also be easily adapted to fit a rectangular frame.

Use Nature As Designer

You should by now be beginning to think about making 'free' designs. A lovely way of doing this – if you are still feeling unsure of yourself – is to use nature itself as designer. What could be more simply effective than an oval picture, backed on green velvet, depicting snowdrops as they appear in a spring garden, or the graceful curves of heather as it blows on moorlands?

This sort of design looks deceptively simple, but be prepared for it to take quite as long to make as something more intricate, because it is so important that it looks just

RIGHT Four ideas are suggested by the rectangular outline of these greetings cards. The first follows half the shape of the frame in an L-shaped design, the largest flower set in the right-angle of the L, and the smallest flowers and dainty foliage softening the outline. On the second card, the focal flower is placed centrally, towards the base of the rectangle, the delicate fern and tiny heuchera leading the eye upwards and outwards. The third card displays a regular design with the pink-edged central daisy claiming immediate attention. The fourth design 'starts' in the top left-hand corner, from where the pendant fuchsias fall to focus attention on the middle of the card. The fuchsia stamens and forget-me-nots then trail away to lead the eye downwards.

BELOW Use nature as designer. These simple designs show snowdrops and heather just as they grow naturally.

right. Snowdrops should be the correct size in relation to each other, their heads hanging at natural angles; and the shapes of the heather stems should look as if they really are growing together. It may be necessary to look through most of your specimens of a particular flower before you find a perfectly natural-looking group, but the end result should make the time spent well worth while.

If you are a botanist at heart, you may well decide that this is the type of flower-work for you. You could then go on to make a variety of botanical pictures of individual species, using both open flowers and buds, together with the correct leaves, and possibly a sliced-through seed-pod. You might even include a washed and pressed section of root. As a final touch, you might want to inscribe the work with the common and Latin names of the flowers.

Balance

Although it is not necessary for a design to be regular in any way, it must be balanced. Balance is not always easy to achieve, and one occasionally looks at a picture, knowing that somethng is wrong although it is not always clear exactly what. A good technique for diagnosing this sort of problem is to turn the picture round and look at it at a different angle. Quite often, a fault that eluded you when the picture was the right way up becomes glaringly obvious when it is upside down.

A good exercise in creating balance is to make a picture entirely from leaves. Leaf pictures are more adaptable than flower designs for this 'all ways round' viewing. Try making one and checking its balance from every angle.

Originality

Sooner or later, you will want to create something original. The joy of working with flowers is that you will certainly be able to do this. If you are artist enough to sketch out ideas for designs, either mentally or on paper, so much the better. But if, like me, you are unable to plan in this way, it is still possible to make designs that are both attractive and original. All you have to do is to allow the flowers them-selves to make the suggetsions. There is no need to start with a clear idea of the sort of design you want to make. You can simply take some carefully pressed flowers and foliage, and place them on a background colour that en-hances their beauty, inside a frame or mount that suits both flowers and background. Then all you have to do is move them around until they suggest ideas.

ABOVE These three designs each use the same flowers and foliage (buttercups, cow parsley and herb Robert) and the same background colour to illustrate three different arrangements in a round frame. The first is a crescent-shaped design which follows the frame outline. The second has a central focal point made up of three main flowers. In the third, the flowers are arranged more naturally as if growing.

Style and Representation

There is a sense in which there are as many different styles as there are pressed-flower artists. And the style of even one individual is likely to keep changing and developing as time passes. It is possible, nevertheless, to identify a number of general stylistic areas. You might like to try your hand at each of these.

The modern style is characterized by its simplicity and concentration on the individual flower. It often uses only one main flower type in any design, together with one or two smaller species which serve to soften the outline and complement the colour of the main blooms. These designs generally have an 'open' appearance, using space to ensure that the individual beauty of each flower is clearly seen.

In contrast to this, the more traditional style commonly uses a mass of overlapping blooms to create a total effect, rather than focusing attention on individual flowers. Many pictures of this sort contain a large number of different species, and are often big enough to accommodate large specimens. The overall effect of this traditional work is full, heavy and grand.

Representational designs are different again. They can vary greatly, ranging from complex and intricately-worked pictures to 'designs' which seem to present themselves ready-made.

There are many beautiful examples of complex representational work depicting such subjects as elegant ladies with sumptuous gowns, fashioned entirely from overlapping delphinium petals; graceful swans, brought to life from the feathery silver leaves of cineraria and silverweed; and the most exquisitely-worked landscapes.

Some of the most original representational work is that which uses seeds in all their subtle varieties of colour, texture and shape to make the most charming and realistic pictures of birds.

It is obvious that an enormous amount of loving care has gone into making these pictures. The outline of the bird is first sketched on to the background card, after which the eyes and beak are fixed into position. Then a small area of glue is applied directly to the card and each seed is carefully placed in position, working from the bottom upwards to ensure that the 'feathers' overlap realistically.

It sometimes happens that simple representations of such subjects as butterflies, birds and trees offer themselves straight from the pages of pressing books. A single petal has only to fall from the five-petalled St John's wort – and there is a 'butterfly' with stamen antennae. If two petals fall from the beautifully-veined ballerina geranium, four 'wings' are again revealed (and, if you are lucky, there will also be two visible sections of calyx in the right position for anten-

ABOVE *In this seed picture, the tawny owl is fashioned mainly from hogweed seeds, with pear-pips (seeds) for eyes, the curved seeds of marigold for 'eyebrows' and cosmos daisies for claws.*

RIGHT *Simply made birds. 1 A 'swan' made from a cranesbill seed pod and silverweed leaves. 2 A Christmas robin with a cherry tree body and clematis tail. 3 More cherry leaf birds in flight.*

nae). It is only one step from this to selecting four suitably-proportioned *Clematis montana* leaves, and making a butterfly with an oaty grass spikelet for a body and fuchsia stamens for antennae.

It is not only insects that 'appear' in this way. The aptly-named cranesbill seed-pod simply asks to be made into a bird's head and neck, and looks effective with the feathery leaves of silverweed forming a swan-like body. Other birds 'grow' on the flowering cherry tree. You have only to look at the feathery outlines of its foliage to imagine a group of birds in flight, and those of its leaves which obligingly turn red on one 'breast' in autumn, make delightful robins when given a seed eye, leaf wing and fanciful clematis seed tail.

You will also discover 'trees' in the pages of pressing books. It is a simple matter to incorporate the lush green fern 'species' into summer landscapes, and those with the bare silver 'branches' into wintry scenes. (And whatever the season, a few grass seed 'birds' could fly around the treetops.)

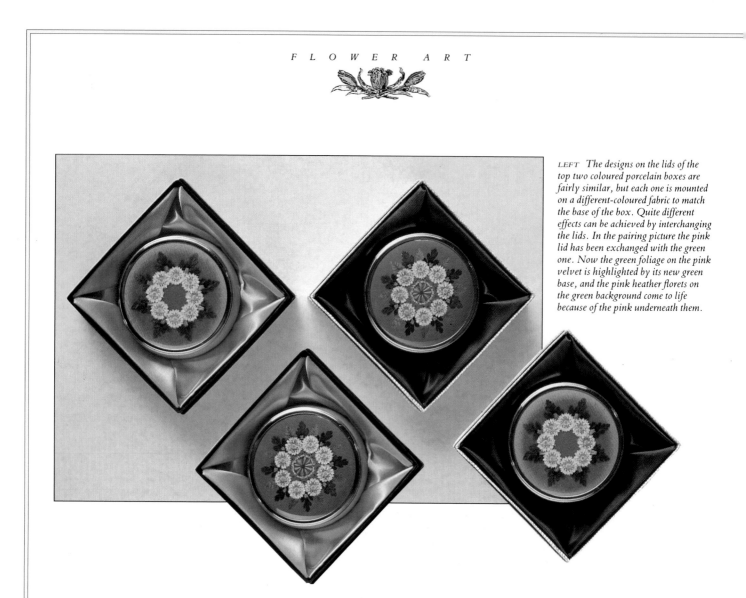

LEFT *The designs on the lids of the top two coloured porcelain boxes are fairly similar, but each one is mounted on a different-coloured fabric to match the base of the box. Quite different effects can be achieved by interchanging the lids. In the pairing picture the pink lid has been exchanged with the green one. Now the green foliage on the pink velvet is highlighted by its new green base, and the pink heather florets on the green background come to life because of the pink underneath them.*

Colour

There are three colour elements to be considered in relation to any design: the colour of the flowers; of the background; and of the frame or setting. Vastly different effects can be achieved by different combinations of these three elements. One of the delights of working with flowers is experimenting with them.

Everyone has different ideas on how to choose flower colours. Successful pictures range from those which imitate the summer herbaceous border in presenting a riot of mixed colours, to those which use the most muted of shades.

Choosing background colour is largely an artistic decision, but it has one technical aspect. Most pressed flowers lose some colour of the years and some fade relatively quickly. It is therefore inadvisable to use very pale backgrounds unless there is a good reason to be confident about the colour fastness of the flowers being used. When – as in the case of celandines – you know that they will lose much of their brilliance during the first year, choose a strong background colour. Experiment, placing the flowers on different backgrounds to find out which combinations best please you.

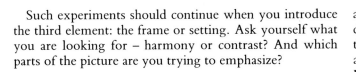

*This design of buttercups, golden rod
and montbretia, and acer leaves follows
the shape of the oval frame.*

Such experiments should continue when you introduce
the third element: the frame or setting. Ask yourself what
you are looking for – harmony or contrast? And which
parts of the picture are you trying to emphasize?

Choice of Frame

The oval frame is perhaps the most attractive for flower
work. It is well proportioned for use with 'growing flower'
designs that follow the contour of the frame. These are not
difficult to make because the shape of the frame can actually
act as a guide when you are arranging the flowers. First
decide upon a focal point – the spot that is going to attract
the eye first. This is usually towards the base of the picture,
and often consists of the largest flowers or group of flowers.
It may be central or slightly off-set, but in either case, the
eye should rest on this point, before being led upwards and
outwards towards the smaller, lighter flowers and foliage
which follow the curve of the frame.

Round frames can also be used effectively with designs
which follow their contours, but like ovals they are versatile
enough to be used in other ways as well.

Rectangular frames or outlines offer similar scope for
design shapes.

USEFUL FLOWERS FOR PRESSING

The fruits and vegetables that we are now able to buy are increasingly international and the same is true of the flowers in florists and nurseries. Cultivated flowers are invariably descended from wild flowers or are actually wild flowers from another part of the world. For example many cultivated lobelias, montbretias and heathers grown in northern temperate countries originated in South Africa; fuchsias have similarly been exported from New Zealand, and the lovely *Helipterum roseum* and several other everlasting flowers from Australia; the flowering currant, heuchera, the *Limnanthes,* larkspur, phlox, hydrangea and golden rod are from North America.

If you are unfamiliar with some of the flowers listed below, identify similar members of the same plant family that grow near you and try pressing them instead. Violets and pansies (Violaceae), vetches (Leguminosae), heathers (Ericaceae) and daisies (Compositae) are all members of families that have a worldwide distribution. (The Composites that I have included in this section should be pressed using the collar method if they are to be used whole.)

In North America, there are many different species of viola. Perhaps the most immediately attractive is the fern-leaved violet, *Viola vittata,* which is rather like *Viola tricolor.* You might also try some of the large number of North American pea plants (Leguminosae) and any heathers that grow in your area. The most obvious Composite to try is *Gaillardia pulchella,* otherwise known as Indian blanket, or, more descriptively, firewheels. Both the swamp rose and the prairie rose should press satisfactorily.

In New Zealand and Australia, there is again considerable potential in the vetch and viola families. In the absence of native heathers, try intead the pink *Epacis impressa* and the smaller-flowered white *E. microphylla.* Any everlasting flower flat enough to press is also a candidate for attention, so it would be well worth trying small specimens of the strawflower or yellow paper daisy, *Helichrysum bracteatum.*

Cultivated Flowers: Spring

ALYSSUM

(Alyssum saxatile)

This is the sweet-smelling yellow alyssum which is often grown together with aubrieta. It is not a marvellous colour-keeper, but is too pretty to pass over completely. Press its minute round buds and tiny, just open, flowers.

SPIRAEA

(Spiraea argula)

A shrub that produces large numbers of tiny white flowers on slender arching stems. Each flower should be snipped off and pressed separately. A little later on in the season look out for *S. bumalda,* which produces clusters of crimson flowers.

POACHED EGG PLANT

(Limnanthes douglasii)

A quickly spreading hardy annual, producing dish-shaped flowers which are easy to press and very attractive. Putting one or more directly on top of another intensifies their delicate colour.

HEUCHERA

(Heuchera sanguinea)

One of the most useful small flowers, and one of the best red ones for keeping colour. The bell-shaped blooms grow many to a stem. Pick them when the lower flowers are fully out and the top ones still in bud, for then the stem is spread enough to be pressed whole.

ANEMONE

(Anemone blanda)

A delicate daisy-like flower with blue or mauve petals surrounding a yellow middle. Choose only those with the deepest colour

PRIMULA

(Primula spp.)

There are many different species of this valuable flower, some of which have a bloom on each stem, whereas others grow in clusters. Most of them are potential 'pressers' and it is well worth while experimenting. The yellow and orange flowers usually press true, while the reds and purples darken. It is advisable to remove the green calyx and to trim off that part of the back of the flower which would otherwise lie behind one of the delicate petals and mark it.

FLOWERING CURRANT

(Ribes sanguineum)

Another spring-flowering shrub, valuable for its small bell-shaped flowers which hang in clusters. Press buds and flowers separately.

DAFFODIL

(Narcissus minimus)

In spite of their three-dimensional shape, ordinary daffodils can be pressed by the usual method. It is probably simpler, however, to stick to those varieties of the extensive *Narcissus* family which can be pressed whole. These include the miniature daffodil, named above, which is small enough to be pressed in profile, and the lovely narcissus, 'Soleil d'or', which has several golden flowers on each stem. The trumpet sections of these flowers are relatively flat and will, if you make a few small snips in them, lie against the outer petals so that you can press them open.

FORGET-ME-NOT

(Myosotis alpestris)

Invaluable, and well worth the trouble of snipping off some of the flowers for separate pressing. This creates uncrowded stems which also press well. The spiral of buds at the top of each stem is particularly attractive.

LONDON PRIDE

(Saxifraga urbium)

This produces sprays of small pink flowers on each stem. Flowers should be pressed separately after the removal of the projecting seedboxes. This is a painstaking process, but you will be rewarded with little pink circles, spotted with deep red, which look delightful in miniature designs together with forget-me-nots. Try also the larger-flowered saxifrages which grow one to a stem. The rosy-coloured ones press beautifully, producing pink, almost translucent petals.

Cultivated Flowers: Summer

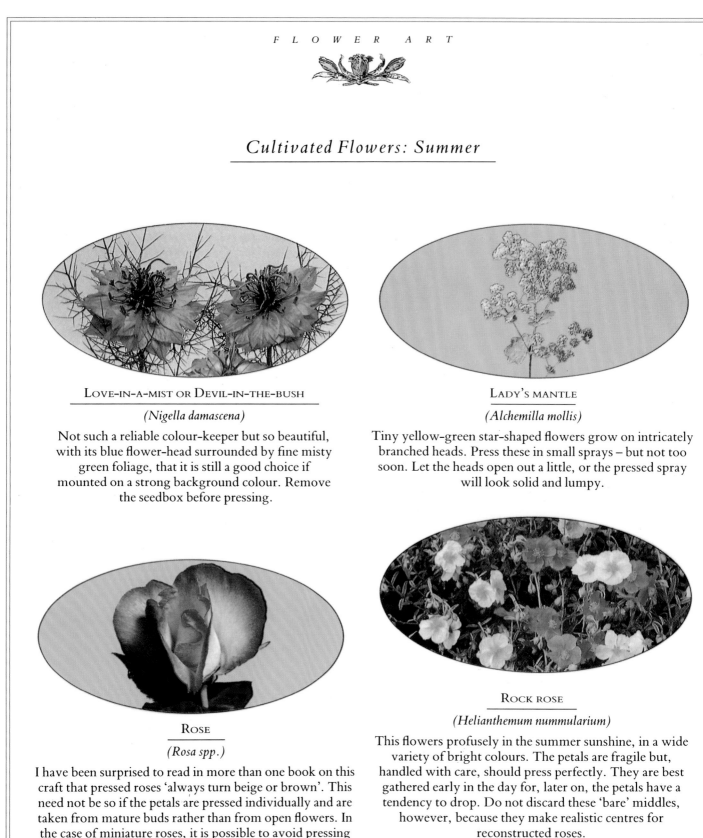

Love-in-a-mist or Devil-in-the-bush

(Nigella damascena)

Not such a reliable colour-keeper but so beautiful, with its blue flower-head surrounded by fine misty green foliage, that it is still a good choice if mounted on a strong background colour. Remove the seedbox before pressing.

Lady's mantle

(Alchemilla mollis)

Tiny yellow-green star-shaped flowers grow on intricately branched heads. Press these in small sprays – but not too soon. Let the heads open out a little, or the pressed spray will look solid and lumpy.

Rock rose

(Helianthemum nummularium)

This flowers profusely in the summer sunshine, in a wide variety of bright colours. The petals are fragile but, handled with care, should press perfectly. They are best gathered early in the day for, later on, the petals have a tendency to drop. Do not discard these 'bare' middles, however, because they make realistic centres for reconstructed roses.

Rose

(Rosa spp.)

I have been surprised to read in more than one book on this craft that pressed roses 'always turn beige or brown'. This need not be so if the petals are pressed individually and are taken from mature buds rather than from open flowers. In the case of miniature roses, it is possible to avoid pressing the petals separately by slicing the buds in two, and pressing each half in profile. The smallest rose of all is the much loved *Rosa farreri persetosa*. This is a single variety, so the tiny buds can actually be pressed whole. They look delightful in simple designs which also use their miniature leaves.

Lobelia

(Lobelia erinus)

Another 'true blue' colour-keeper. Pick only a few at a time for its petals curl quickly.

GYPSOPHILA OR BABIES' BREATH

(Gypsophila paniculata)

These sprays of tiny white flowers are very useful as delicate 'space fillers' to soften the outline of designs.

LARKSPUR

(Delphinium consolida)

More useful than its perennial relative, this annual has an even bigger range of colours which are bright, press 'true', and do not fade. Could you ask for more?

PANSY

(Viola tricolor hortensis)

These are found in many different sizes and colours. (Yellow flowers keep their colour particularly well.) My preference is for the smaller ones and those with the most defined 'faces'.

GRANDMOTHER'S PINCUSHION

(Astrantia carniolica)

The true flowers of this interesting plant are tiny, but the surrounding bracts look like the petals of a larger flower. These bracts may be white and green, pink or a maroon-red. Their pointed shape gives them a geometric appearance, like the points of a compass.

DELPHINIUM

(Delphinium elatum)

This is a tall perennial with colours varying from pale blue to deep mauve. It proudly contradicts the fallacy that blue flowers do not keep their colour. (I have seen pictures of pages taken from a scrapbook over 100 years old in which the delphiniums are still blue!) Each flower on the stem should be pressed individually, but may still be rather large for many designs. If this is the case, wait for smaller flowers on the side-shoots, or consider presssing the petals separately.

CLARY

(Salvia horminum)

This is another plant with insignificant flowers whose beauty is in its bracts. These are pink and purple and keep colour well. They can be used in designs as the 'petals' of imaginary flowers.

Peruvian lily

(Alstroemeria aurantiaca)

This lovely perennial, which grows in a variety of colours, is a good example of a three-dimensional flower whose individual petals are so beautiful that it is really worth while pressing them separately, prior to reconstructing them into imaginary two-dimensional flowers. Unfortunately these flowers are more frequently seen in florists' shops than in gardens – but perhaps this is something we should try to change, for they are not difficult to grow and the species named above is hardy.

Phlox or Pride of texas

(Phlox drummondii)

The short annual species of phlox, each stem of which bears many flowers in dense heads. Pick the florets singly and trim off the backs. The various colours undergo subtle changes during pressing.

St John's wort

(Hypericum elatum)

This shrub species produces masses of small, yellow, dish-shaped flowers, measuring about 1in (2.5cm) across and having a lovely central boss of golden stamens. Remove the seedbox before pressing. The stamens are even more spectacular on the shorter but larger-flowered *H. calycinum,* known as the rose of Sharon or Aaron's beard.

Hydrangea

(Hydrangea spp.)

Many species of this plant are excellent for pressing. The pinks, blues, and even the underdeveloped greens press well once the florets have been separated from the densely-flowering heads.

Fuchsia

(Fuchsia magellanica)

The flowers of this bushy shrub are smaller and less moisture-laden than those of most of its exotic relatives. These are the qualities which make it the hardiest of the fuchsias and the best for pressing. Press the lovely pendant flowers in profile, leaving them on their curving stems and taking care to arrange the petals evenly. The scarlet stamens are so striking that you might occasionally choose to use them separated from the flower (for instance as butterfly antennae).

Montbretia

(Crocosmia x crocosmiiflora)

Pick these graceful curving stems when most of the flowers are still in bud. They then retain their deep, orange colour. Any of the trumpet-shaped flowers which are already out may be pressed separately, open or in profile.

Cultivated Flowers: Autumn and Winter

HEATHER

(Erica carnea)

The various winter-flowering heathers provide wonderful splashes of colour at a time when this is otherwise in short supply. The pink varieties are particularly attractive. The flower spikes can be pressed whole, but what comes out of the press tend to be too solid-looking to use as it is. So discard the woody stems and spiky leaves, which usually drop off anyway, and use only the tiny bright pink flowers.

SNOWDROP

(Galanthus nivalis)

Use only the 'single-skirted' varieties and press in bud or profile. Do not try to press them open because this looks unnatural. Consider using them with the spiky white-lined leaves of the crocus.

GOLDEN ROD

(Solidago spp.)

Remove the curved plumes of tiny golden flowers from the tall stems. These may then be used whole, or separately for miniature designs.

Everlastings

Anaphalis, sea lavender and helipterum, are all of the 'everlasting' type more usually seen in three-dimensional dried-flower arrangements. They are more or less dry when picked, and need only to be hung up for a week or two in a warm, airy place to complete the process. They then need pressing very briefly just to flatten them, and they can subsequently be relied upon to retain colour for years. The best everlasting specimens for pressing are, of course, those which are not too bulky.

SEA LAVENDER OR STATICE

(Limonium sinuatum)

This grows in a variety of bright colours. Press each of the florets separately.

ANAPHALIS OR PEARLY EVERLASTING

(Anaphalis yedoensis)

Clusters of pearly white flowers grow on a single stem. When they are dry, remove the seed heads from the middle of each flower to reveal the beautifully detailed, green-centred faces. Press each flower separately.

HELIPTERUM

(Helipterum roseum)

A beautiful pink daisy-like flower with papery-dry petals.

Wild Flowers

Never pick rare flowers. Never pick common flowers from places where they are scarce or protected. Remember that if you pick all this year's crop, there will be no seeds for next year. However abundant the flowers may be, never pick more than you need.

Fortunately, most of the best wild flowers for pressing are the very common ones. There are, however, one or two exceptions. It is now unusual, for example, to come across large numbers of primroses or heartsease (wild pansies) in the countryside.

It is even more important with wild flowers to have some idea about when to expect them because, unlike their cultivated counterparts, many wild flowers may be too far away to present a daily visual reminder that now is the time to gather them, and some of them have a relatively short season.

COLTSFOOT

(Tussilago farfara)

This is the only one of the dandelion-type flowers to press satisfactorily because, unlike the others, it has a flat middle. It is therefore easy to spread the surrounding spiky 'petals' evenly. Again, it is worth considering using its equally attractive underside.

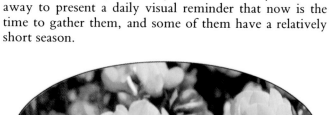

BIRD'S FOOT TREFOIL

(Lotus corniculatus)

An attractive meadow flower, best pressed in bud because the deep yellow buds are richer in colour and sometimes, if you are lucky, tipped with red. This is a member of the vetch family, or Leguminosae, many of whose members, yellow or purple, are well worth considering for pressing.

CELANDINE

(Ranunculus ficaria)

These brilliant yellow starry flowers open their glossy petals to reflect the spring sunshine. They will pale down after a year or so to a lemony-cream colour, but they are so beautiful in form that, if mounted against a dark background, they will still be attractive.

ELDERFLOWER

(Sambucus nigra)

These frothy, cream flower-heads have many florets to a stem. Heads may be pressed complete or in sprays. Used individually or in clusters in a design, the creamy-beige flowers add delicacy to your work.

DOG ROSE

(Rosa canina)

This charmingly simple wild rose is unlike its lusher, fuller-petalled garden relatives in that it can be pressed whole. Remove the seedbox from behind the flower.

COW PARSLEY

(Anthriscus sylvestris)

This is just one of the many useful species of the Umbellifer family. Others to look out for are fool's parsley, earthnut, burnet saxifrage, rough chervil and wild carrot. All have branched umbels, each topped with 'rays' or clusters of tiny flowers. To make a representation of such intricate structures in paint, embroidery or lace would indeed be work for a patient artist. But nature makes it easy for the flower-presser by offering us this family of plants, the different members of which adorn the countryside throughout the late spring and summer. Press whole umbels or separate rays.

HEATHER

(Calluna vulgaris)

This common wild variety is, perhaps, preferable to its stiffer cultivated counterparts. It grows on moorland and you can almost see the wind in the graceful curves of its stems. Its foliage, too, is attractive and does not drop.

DAISY

(Bellis perennis)

This most indispensable of all wild flowers certainly lives up to its Latin name, for not only does it recur profusely year after year, it also has a long season, in many areas appearing before most flowers we would particularly associate with spring, and continuing to bloom well into the autumn. Moreover, it is an ideal candidate for pressing. The best specimens are those with pink-edged petals (probably the result of cross-pollination with the cultivated varieties).

BUTTERCUP

(Ranunculus acris)

Beautiful and easy to press, buttercups grow abundantly in many areas. Avoid roadside flowers if possible, for they are usually dusty. *R. repens* is the equally attractive creeping buttercup.

Foliage

It is possible to make effective designs using leaves only, but though flower pictures without foliage may be pretty, they are bound to look unnatural – for where can flowers ever be seen growing in the absence of greenery?

It follows, therefore, that it is necessary to press a good selection of leaves. As with flowers there are some which press better than others and some general guidelines may be given regarding which these are. Types of leaves to avoid are the fleshy ones, like those of African violet; needles, like those of pine or many of the cultivated heathers; and thick evergreens, such as laurel, which refuse to dry out properly. Most other types of leaves press successfully, and the choice depends on finding specimens that are manageably small, interesting in shape and attractive in colour.

HERB ROBERT
(Geranium robertianum)

The small purple flowers of this plant are fairly ordinary, but the beautifully-shaped, slightly hairy leaves are invaluable. They are often made even more attractive in the latter part of the year by a tinge of red.

EARTHNUT
(Conopodium majus)

Many members of the Umbellifer family have delicate leaves which press well. This is the most dainty, especially when gathered in the spring, before the white flowers appear. Press as soon as possible after picking, or the leafy sprays tend to wilt and close up.

COMMON MEADOW RUE
(Thalictrum flavum)

The tiny yellow flowers are insignificant but the leaves are beautifully angular. Press both the bright green leaves of midsummer and those which turn yellow as the plant approaches the end of its season.

SILVERWEED
(Potentilla anserina)

This is another indispensable plant, whose feather-edged leaves are grey-green on top and silver underneath. They can be used whole in large designs and are equally beautiful when segmented into smaller pieces. Silver-leaved plants are generally useful for the attractive variation they bring to designs and because they do not change colour. Cultivated cineraria and pyrethrum also offer particularly beautiful silver leaves.

VIRGINIA CREEPER
(Parthenocissus quinquefolia)

These beautifully shaped leaves are at their best in their glorious autumn colours.

PYRETHRUM
(Chrysanthemum/Pyrethrum ptarmica folium)

Also known as silver feather, this plant has intricately-shaped leaves which can be used whole or separated into small sections for use in miniature designs.

CLEMATIS
(Clematis montana)

The young leaves turn a striking black when pressed.

ECCREMOCARPUS OR CHILEAN GLORY FLOWER
(Eccremocarpus scaber)

A useful annual climber, whose tubular orange flowers are best left alone but whose interestingly-shaped leaves also turn black on pressing.

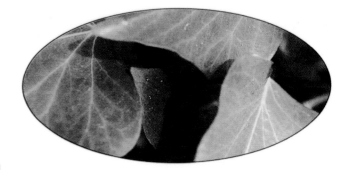

COMMON IVY OR ENGLISH IVY
(Hedera helix)

Press the smaller leaves of the dark green varieties which keep colour better than the variegated ones.

CINERARIA
(Cineraria maritima)

The 'Silver dust' variety has delicate fern-like leaves.

The Leaves of Trees

MAPLE

(Acer spp.)

All the members of the large acer family of trees and shrubs are grown for their ornamental foliage, and produce a variety of beautiful shapes and colours.

BEECH

(Fagus sylvatica)

Both the green and copper varieties are best pressed in spring. The young leaves of the copper beech give an autumn feel to designs.

OAK OR ENGLISH OAK

(Quercus pedunculata)

Press the immature leaves in spring time.

SUMACH

(Rhus spp.)

Best picked in autumn, when the leaves turn brilliant orange or scarlet. Look for smaller leaves on the creeping suckers.

FLOWERING CHERRY

(Prunus spp.)

There are many varieties of these lovely trees. The leaves of most of them are beautiful in autumn and best collected just before they drop. Their lovely colours, shape and feathery outline make these leaves perfect for Christmas card 'robins'.

Other Plant Material

SEEDS

The loveliest are probably the feathery whirls produced by many of the different varieties of clematis. The winged seeds of the sycamore maple (Acer pseudoplatanus) can also be used to make similar simple representations of moths' wings. Some 'natural artists' work only in this medium.

FERNS

Many types of fern press satisfactorily. Three that are used regularly are the delicate maiden-hair fern (Adiantum capillus-veneris) with its lovely sprays of green, and two bigger ferns: the common bracken or brake (Pteridium aquilinum) and the prettier hay-scented buckler fern (Dryopteris aemula). Pick young fronds, but consider splitting them into more manageable sizes before pressing.

GRASSES

Most grasses press well because they are fairly dry to start with. The delicate grasses are perhaps the most useful because they help to achieve a lovely soft outline when used for filling the spaces around a design. But try to press a variety of specimens: green and brown; straight and curved; solid and feathery.

SEED-PODS

There are several of these which can be attractively used in two-dimensional designs. Honesty (Lunaria annua) produces shiny silver discs when the stems have been dried and the dark outer pods removed. Herb Robert, being a member of the cranesbill family, produces a seed-pod illustrating that name. Even the seedbox of the common poppy (Papaver rhoeas), though three-dimensional as a whole, can create a beautiful little 'wooden flower' if its fluted top is carefully sliced off.

MOSSES

Mosses are especially useful in miniature designs, where small, curving pieces can create the effect that a combination of curved stems and leaves might have made in a larger design. It is not until one begins collecting for the press that one realizes how many different shapes, sizes and shades of moss there are.

Drying:

TECHNIQUES IN DRYING

*J*ust as with preserving flowers and plants, drying plant material means that you always have something on hand with which to create a flower arrangement. There are two major methods of drying: drying flat and drying by hanging in bunches.

Drying Flat

This is the most commonly used method of drying flowers (either complete blooms or single petals), especially if they are to be used for other than decorative purposes. Petals should be detached carefully to avoid damaging or bruising them. Spread the petals and whole blooms out in a single layer on slatted shelves or between two sheets of newspaper in an airing cupboard, on newspaper and covered in muslin on trays in a warm, dry cupboard or near a central heating boiler. Prop the tray up on cotton reels to let the air circulate underneath if necessary. If you have an accessible attic, you could lay the flowers on muslin or net suspended, hammock-fashion, from the rafters. Drying may take from four to 10 days according to the flower and the humidity. They are ready when they feel crisp and rustle gently, like dry leaves, when lightly handled. To check whether they are completely dry, put one or two in a small air-tight jar and leave for a day or two. If condensation appears on the sides of the jar or on the bottom the flowers need to be dried a little more.

Flowers can also be dried in a plate-warming drawer or an ordinary oven, set to the lowest possible heat with the oven door propped open. This method will take only about an hour, but it requires more vigilance. Make sure the flowers do not become too warm – the temperature should be no higher than blood heat.

A microwave oven can also be used. Spread the petals or blooms out between sheets of absorbent paper and microwave for a minute, turning them over halfway through the drying process.

The small, electrically-powered home herb driers that are now available can also be used for drying flowers.

Hanging in Bunches

To dry flowers successfully by suspending them in bunches requires an atmosphere that is completely dry. There must be adequate ventilation and a good circulation of air, the temperature must be right and the flowers must be away from direct sunlight.

Not all flowers can be dried successfully. 'Everlasting' flowers change least when dried. Long-stemmed annual and perennial delphiniums, astilbe, lavender pink heathers, sea heathers, and leek and onion flower heads are some of the other most popular choices.

Group the flowers into bunches that are not too large so that the air can circulate, then tie the bunches fairly tightly, leaving a loop to hang them from. Suspend them, heads downwards, from separate hooks, a line or coathanger.

Methodology

Using a desiccant, such as powdered borax, sand, silica gel and proprietary mixtures, is the best way of preserving flowers that are to be used for ornamental purposes as it will remove the moisture from the flowers effectively and preserve the structure, shape and colour of petals that would be spoilt by the other methods of drying.

Silica gel crystals, available from chemists, are the most expensive desiccant. They can be crushed with a rolling pin to reduce the size of the crystals. Proprietory names for fine crystals are Lasting Flower and Flora-D Hydrate. Silica gel is the fastest-acting desiccant, producing dried blooms in only one to three days. The colour of the flowers is therefore good but there is a tendency for them to become brittle if left in the desiccant for too long.

The silica gel mixture itself can be used over and over again, if after each application it is slowly dried out in a low-temperature oven. When you see blue crystals emerging, you know that the mixture has been reactivated.

Alum and borax can also be bought from the chemist and these are inexpensive. They are particularly good for delicate petals. Allow seven to 10 days for the drying process. Borax often then needs a little encouragement to persuade it to come away from the dried flowers.

ABOVE *1 To wire flower heads before drying, remove most of the stem and push stub wire through the flower centre. Coil the extra wire around the base of the flower for support.*

ABOVE *2 Cover the bottom of a deep, airtight container with the desiccant. Lay the flowers on it according to their shape and size – smaller flowers face down, larger ones on their sides.*

LEFT *3 Gently sift or pour the desiccant over the flowers, allowing it to fall between the petals and into the flower centre. Continue until the flowers are completely covered.*

The blooms can be given false stems after drying by carefully inserting florists' wire or even pipe cleaners (although these are not as good). Flower heads are easier to wire before drying. Cut off most of the stem then push a piece of wire down through the centre of the flower, or, if easier, depending on the bloom, push the wire up through the stem end. Coil the wire round neatly below the flower to support it.

Cover the base of a large, deep tin, such as a biscuit tin, with about ½–1 in (1.5–2.5 cm) of desiccant, carefully smoothing out any lumps. Lay petals or flowers without stems on the desiccant in accordance with their shape – for example, pansies and buttercups should be placed face down while fragile flowers like hollyhocks should be laid on their sides. If the flowers have stems place a wire mesh over or in the tin and insert the flowers, heads uppermost. Gently sift the desiccant around the flowers then carefully let it fall naturally in between the petals and right into the centre of each bloom, using a fine brush or skewer if necessary to ease it into place, until the blooms are completely covered. Trumpet-shaped flowers are an exception, they should be filled with desiccant before being covered. Cover the tin with an airtight lid then leave it somewhere warm, dark and dry.

The texture and thickness of the petals and the density of the blooms will govern the length of time they will take to dry. Lawn daisies, for example, should be ready in two days whereas African marigolds need two weeks.

Carefully pour off the desiccant, allowing the petals and flowers to drop into your hand. If the flowers feel papery with no signs of dampness they are sufficiently dry. If they do not, dry them for a little longer.

Brush away any remaining desiccant with the point of a fine brush. Any petals that have come away from complete heads can be stuck back in place using a transparent glue and a wooden cocktail stick. Add a few crystals of silica gel to the container if the flowers or petals are to be stored just in case there is any rogue moisture.

RIGHT *6 When drying intricate or delicate flowers, it may be necessary to brush away any remaining desiccant between the petals with the point of a fine brush.*

ABOVE *4 Close the container with an airtight lid and leave in a warm, dry place. When the crystals turn from blue to white, the flower moisture has been absorbed.*

ABOVE *5 Carefully pour off the desiccant. If the flowers are ready, they will feel papery and completely dry. If not, replace them in the crystals for a little longer.*

DRIED FLOWER ARRANGEMENTS

*I*n the winter months, when there are few fresh flowers to work with, dried flowers can provide particularly welcome decoration for the home. Large designs can fill empty fireplaces or the unused corners of rooms, and smaller arrangements can be made as centre-pieces for occasional tables or mantlepieces. It is well worth putting time and trouble into your designs, since they will continue to look appealing for many months after you complete them.

With dried material, you can be very inventive in choosing containers since there is no problem of water seepage to consider. Pieces of driftwood, weathered wood and bark found on rambles might be employed, perhaps, or, for something more unusual, you could buy lengths of metal piping.

Dried flowers can also be used to decorate small boxes or wastepaper baskets, and they can make delightful pictures to hang on the wall. Miniatures can be really charming, but here it is important to choose material in the right proportion and you will need tweezers to set the material in place. This may seem slow exercise but it can be very satisfying to complete such a picture. Old frames, which can be cleaned and resprayed, are often to be found in salerooms.

A clear glass dome placed over an arrangement of dried flowers looks very effective and provides the additional benefit of protecting the flowers from dust. Make the found-ation for the arrangement out of foam or fine wire mesh formed to a suitable shape then insert flowers to build up an attractive display.

Useful Flowers for Dried Arrangements

There is always a vast and exciting choice of dried materials available from the florists, but if you grow your own flowers many of them can be dried very easily at home.

Some subjects dry more attractively than others. For example, if delphiniums are cut just before maturity, they will eventually dry out keeping an almost perfect colour. They are best cut when about half the spikes show full colour. They should then be stood in about 2in (5cm) of water and allowed to condition thoroughly. Then hang them upside-down in a dry, draught-free place until they gradually dry out. A light coating with clear spray will help to keep the florets in place.

ACHILLEA retains its golden colour for several years.

HELICHRYSUMS AND STATICE are very popular as dried materials. They supply a wonderful variety of both colour and form. For people who grow their own helichrysums, remember to insert a wire through the flower head as soon as it is cut as, once it dries, it becomes almost too hard to pierce. Try to insert the wire up through a short stem so that it does not show. Then hang the flowers upside-down in bunches ready for using in your winter arrangements.

HYDRANGEAS also keep their colour, particularly the green and red varieties, but the pale blue variety turns brown, although it is useful for masking the foam. It is best to strip the foliage from hydrangeas before leaving them to dry out.

MOLUCELLA bleaches to a delicate cream tint as it gradually dries. Arranged with grasses or fabric flower, it makes very elegant line material and is long lasting.

ROSES, also, can be dried on their natural stems, while almost any flower head can be quickly and successfully dried in silica gel. You need quite a large quantity, for the heads should be arranged in layers and copiously covered with the gel. This is available from most good chemist shops or from specialist suppliers of flower arranging materials.

LEFT This is a 'petite' arrangement, which is defined as one under 9in (23cm) in size. The shell container was picked up on the beach and glued to another shell for use as a base.

Materials: shell container, soaked floral foam. Dried flowers of dyed sea lavender, xeranthemum, statice, tansy, santolina; hare's-tail grass.

1 Insert the sea lavender to give a curving outline. 2 Add the xeranthemums to the outside and over the rim. 3 Add the statice, tansy and santolina to the centre. 4 Fill in with a few hare's-tails and a little more sea lavender.

LEFT Design in sepia.

Materials: marble container, two photos without frames, brown base, cream lace drape, stick in bottle, modelling clay, soaked floral foam in candle-cup placed on top of marble container.

Glycerined plant material including dock, foxglove, seedheads, beech, laurel, yew, eucalyptus, Grevillea robusta; dried flowers of statice, helichrysum, gypsophila (baby's breath); a few skeletonized magnolia leaves; hare's-tail and pampas grasses.

1 Insert dock, hare's-tail and pampas to give a triangular outline. 2 Add foxglove seedheads, statice and helichrysum. 3 Add a few more hare's-tails lower down. 4 Place skeletonized magnolia beech and laurel near the middle, along with a few more flowers. 5 Fill in the gaps with small pieces of eucalyptus, grevillea and gypsophila. 6 Arrange laurel leaves so that they flow over the rim with the magnolias and pampas. 7 Place on the base, which has been positioned on the cream lace drape. The material is held up at the back by a stick secured in a bottle with modelling clay. Add the photographs to complete the design.

BELOW LEFT This is a design interpreting wood-carving. The wood-like structure of the various pods helps to further the theme, and the different shades of brown are the varying colours of woods.

Materials: tin can with dry floral foam, wood slice. Dried and preserved material, including poinciana pods, coconut spathes, proteas, tulip seedheads, eucalyptus, cones, beech leaves.

1 Insert a large poinciana pod and coconut spathe at the back. 2 Add proteas and tulip pods, and bring other material to form a slightly curving outline. 3 Fill in with the heavy plant material at the centre, and a few preserved leaves to fill in the gaps. 4 Place to one side on the wooden slab.

The Language of Flowers

From Victorian times, and in some cases even earlier, specific flowers when given as a gift have been credited with 'secret' meanings. Such meanings may accordingly be related to the emotions of the giver as aroused by the recipient. Several of the meanings of individual flowers have changed somewhat over the decades, but in general the list retains a considerable element of the traditional.

ACACIA · *secret love*

ALMOND BLOSSOM · *hope*

AMARYLLIS · *pride, splendid beauty*

ANEMONE · *forsaken*

APPLE BLOSSOM · *preference*

BELLFLOWER, WHITE · *gratitude*

BLUEBELL · *constancy*

BROOM · *humility*

CAMELLIA, RED · *unpretending excellence*

CAMELLIA, WHITE · *perfected excellence*

CARNATION, RED · *alas for my poor heart*

CARNATION, STRIPED · *refusal*

CHAMOMILE · *patience*

CHRYSANTHEMUM, RED · *I love*

CLEMATIS · *mental beauty, purity*

COLUMBINE · *folly*

DAISY · *innocence*

ELDERFLOWER · *compassion, consolation*

EVERLASTING FLOWER · *unfading memory*

FORGET-ME-NOT · *fidelity, true love*

HAWTHORN BLOSSOM · *hope*

HEARTSEASE · *remembrance*

HIBISCUS · *delicate beauty*

HONEYSUCKLE · *devotion*

HYACINTH · *unobtrusive loveliness*

HYACINTH, BLUE · *constancy*

JASMINE, WHITE · *amiability*

JASMINE, YELLOW · *happiness, grace and elegance*

JONQUIL · *I desire a return of affection*

LAVENDER · *silence*

LILAC, PURPLE · *first emotions of love*

LILAC, WHITE · *youthful innocence*

LILY · *purity*

LILY-OF-THE-VALLEY · *purity, return of happiness*

MAGNOLIA · *grief*

MARIGOLD · *joy*

MICHAELMAS DAISY · *farewell*

MIGNONETTE · *your qualities are supreme*

NASTURTIUM · *patriotism*

ORANGE BLOSSOM · *purity and loveliness*

PANSIES · *love, thought*

PEONY · *bashfulness*

PINKS · *love*

POPPY, RED · *consolation*

PRIMROSE · *early youth*

ROSE · *love*

ROSE, MUSK · *capricious beauty*

ROSEBUD · *pure and lovely*

ROSEMARY · *remembrance*

SNOWDROP · *hope*

STOCK · *lasting beauty*

SWEET WILLIAM · *gallantry*

TULIP · *love*

VIOLET · *modesty*

WALLFLOWER · *fidelity in adversity*

ZINNIA · *thoughts of absent friends*

Flowers in Church

WEDDING FLOWER ARRANGEMENTS AND POSIES

RIGHT Wedding pew end.
Materials: *Soaked floral foam in container with handle, taped for security; ribbon loop and ribbon tail, wire. Cupressus (cypress), privet, spray carnations.*
  1 Make a framework all around the container with the cupressus, making it longer at the end opposite the handle. 2 Add the privet in between. 3 Insert the buds of long flowers at the end opposite the handle, and, cutting the carnations fairly short, fill in with them at the side and centre. 4 Add the ribbon loops and fill in the gaps with the privet. 5 Fold the ribbon tail nearly in half, and twist a stub wire around the fold; then push at the back into the foam. 6 Cut the ends into a 'V' shape to finish.

RIGHT The classic style, unashamedly expensive when made up in lily-of-the-valley, stephanotis and white roses. These are all traditional bridal flowers, but there is no reason why the same shape should not be copied in many other flowers.

The Bridal Bouquet

Originally, all bouquets were loose natural bunches or tightly-packed nosegays simply tied and held in the hand. In the late eighteenth and nineteenth centuries they became very large and very heavy. Presumably this was in line with the upsurge of interest in horticulture at the time when many brides were almost submerged by cascades of ferns.

FAR RIGHT Bridesmaid's posy.
Materials: *Soaked floral foam, posy holder, posy frill, narrow ribbon for handle, wider ribbon for loops and tail, thin wire, stub wire, gutta-percha. Ivy leaves, roses, spray carnations.*
  1 Push the posy frill on to the handle of the holder until it reaches the top. 2 Bind the handle with the narrow ribbon, and twist a small piece of thin wire tightly around the top to secure the ribbon. Tie on the tail over the wire. 3 Place small ivy leaves around the rim of the holder with wired loops finished with gutta. 4 Add a rose at the centre, and place four more lower down at equal distances around it. 5 Add carnations in between the roses and near the base of the holder. 6 Fill in the gaps with more carnations and rose leaves.

However, in the early 1950s, bouquets began to diminish in size and the technique of making them became far more precise and delicate. Many were miniature works of art. Professional designers were able to do this type of work because they had access to better materials – finer wires, different coloured binding tape and ribbons in a multitude of colours, widths and designs.

Even so, the basic form was much the same. That is, flowers on single stems of taped 'stems', built into a design that could comfortably be held in one hand.

A CLASSIC SHOWER OR WATERFALL shape is still very popular. It is adaptable to almost any type of flower, is easy to hold and looks elegant.

THE SEMI-CRESCENT design is an extremely graceful bouquet. It is just as effective with simple flowers on their natural stems as with 'special wedding' flowers which have to be wired into trails.

THE FULL-CRESCENT is another popular variation, particularly suitable to accompany brides with long, full-skirted gowns.

Whether the bouquet has ribbon trails or not, it should always be neatly finished at the back with a small bow and a comfortable ribbon handle.

All brides deserve lovely flowers for their special day. But never be confused by the vast choice of style and colour, for while the materials will vary considerably from season to season, the basic shapes remain constant. First of all, decide what type of bouquet you would like, and, if possible, plan the colour and shape of the bridesmaids' flowers and any table decorations at the same time. In this way, all the wedding floral decorations will harmonize.

The Bridesmaids

The bridesmaids and flower girls complete the wedding picture. Happily, there is a wide selection of flowers and designs for them to choose from.

Bascades resemble baskets of flowers (although they are actually designed like small bouquets with a ribboned handle), and they can be copied in any size to suit both child attendants and taller bridesmaids. A head-dress to match in either real or fabric flowers, completes the effect.

If the flowers seem limp after the wedding, immerse the bouquet completely in cold water overnight.

Pressing a Bridal Bouquet

Many brides wish to preserve their bouquets. One way of doing this is to press the flowers and make a picture from them. A few hints are given below on how to do this successfully.

The bride's primary concern is obviously to choose flowers that make a beautiful bouquet and suit the colour theme of the wedding. If they are eventually destined for the press, however, some prior consideration should also be given to this fact. Flowers such as orchids or large lilies, for example, do not press satisfactorily, whereas many other traditional bouquet flowers do perfectly well. These include rosebuds, carnations, freesia, alstroemeria, lily-of-the-valley, stephanotis (Madagascar jasmine), heather and the dainty and ever-popular gypsophila (baby's breath). Most of the varied foliage commonly found in wedding bouquets also presses satisfactorily, although asparagus fern is not a marvellous colour-keeper, and its 'needles' have a tendency to drop.

Persuade the florist making the bouquet not to wire every single flower and leaf. All the stems will be wired – which need present no problem – but if each rosebud is liberally stapled to prevent the flower from opening, and every ivy leaf wired to hold it in exactly the right position, then the eventual picture will have the wedding bouquet 'trademark' of two little holes through every rose petal and leaf.

Once it has served its decorative purpose, the bouquet should be dismantled and pressed as soon as possible. It can, if necessary, be kept fresh until the following morning by putting it carefully into a large plastic bag which is then inflated and sealed with a flexible tie. The bag should be stored in a cool place. The bottom of a refrigerator will do admirably, as long as there is no risk of petals being frozen. Do not be tempted, at any stage, to spray the flowers with water in an attempt to keep them fresh. This is distinctly unhelpful, for one of the aims in pressing flowers is to dry them out as quickly as possible.

ABOVE LEFT A full-crescent bouquet of spray chrysanthemums, underlined with gold braid loops of varying sizes. The flowers have conveniently hollow stems so that a fine supporting wire can be inserted without damaging the flower.

ABOVE The rose-coloured velvet background and the mahogany frame used for this bouquet picture blend with the flower colours and have a suitably 'traditional' feel.

BELOW LEFT A tiny baskette or bascade which is, in effect, two large corsages with very long handles which are covered with ribbon and joined firmly together at the centre.

ABOVE This wedding photograph shows the original bouquet from which the picture on the right was subsequently made.

In order to prepare the bouquet for pressing, carefully detach each flower and leaf from its wired stem and remove any staples from rosebuds. Select only the best specimens for pressing. The less perfect ones can be set aside, perhaps, for the preparation of a sweet-smelling *pot pourri*.

Some flowers need no preparation at all. Lily-of-the-valley and heather, for example, can both be pressed just as they are, and gypsophila needs only to be divided into manageable sprays. Stephanotis (Madagascar jasmine) stems need separating into individual flowers, as do freesia, whose curving clusters of buds may, however, be pressed as a group. Other flowers – like roses, carnations and alstroemeria – must have each petal removed. Remember that the sepals of both roses and carnations should also be pressed for the later reconstruction of 'buds'.

The separate petals are delicate, so when using a press, remember to include additional sheets of blotting paper to prevent the corrugations of the card from imprinting themselves on the petals. You might alternatively prefer to press these specimens in a well-weighted book. Roses and carnations are particularly prone to mildew, so it is a good idea to keep the press (or book) in a warm, dry place for the first few days. All the flowers should be ready for use in about six weeks.

Remember when choosing a frame that because a bouquet normally consists of relatively large flowers, you really need a large design area.

Choose a background colour that both reflects the colour theme of the wedding and enhances the flowers. If the bride's and the bridesmaids' dresses have been specially made and there is any leftover fabric, it may be possible to use this as background.

You may also like to make some additional small designs in such settings as little oval watch-top frames or hand-turned mahogany boxes, as souvenirs for bridesmaids, mothers and grandmothers.

Wedding Prayer-book Spray

Instead of the traditional wedding bouquet, some brides prefer to carry a white bible or prayer book, with a small spray of flowers attached.

In effect, the spray follows the same kind of design as a bouquet and should be made in proportion to the size of the book. If it is too large, the whole effect is lost.

Ribbon markers are a matter for personal preference. One is usually passed through the page at the beginning of the Marriage Service and the other across the inside of the cover. These ribbons can look very attractive either left plain or decorated with tiny fresh flower heads.

Wedding Cake Decoration

If possible, the bridal cake top should match, or at least blend with some of the flowers in the bridal bouquet. If the bouquet is made with large flowers, such as red roses, then obviously this is not feasible, but sometimes a flower can be diminished by using just a few petals and joining them in small trails as mini-flowers.

You could even place a favourite vase on top of the cake and create a design on natural stems if the flowers are suitable. The cake top design should be kept as delicate as possible and in proportion to the final overall size and height of the cake.

The auto-corso has a suction base (ABOVE) on which soaked foam is secured (FAR LEFT).

FAR LEFT BOTTOM. This classic head-dress is attached to a small hair comb. You can secure it with silver wire or with clear adhesive.

FAR LEFT TOP. Anchor the spray firmly to the prayer book so that it fits closely to the cover.

LEFT. The cake top is designed to match the all-white classic bouquet on page 114. Built in accordance with the five-point motif, all the wire 'stems' are bound at one point and then bound together to form one stem that neatly fits into the silver vase.

RIGHT. Horizontal-style flower arrangement for the wedding car built on an 'auto-corso' base.

Bridesmaids' Parasols

For a summer country wedding, flower-decorated parasols would make charming accessories for the bridesmaids. They are quite lightweight to carry and can be closed for the ceremony. This should have no effect on the flower trimming provided it is done carefully. It is, of course, advisable to let your florist know whether you would like the parasol to be used both open and closed and then the trimming can be arranged accordingly.

Bridal Car Decoration

Decorating the bridal car can also contribute to the festivity of the occasion. The Oasis company has produced a suction base called an auto-corso which can be arranged in exactly the same manner as a horizontal-style flower arrangement. There can be no damage to coachwork as the base is rubber. The decoration can be fixed either to one wing or to the bonnet, attached to water-resistant ribbons stretched from either side of the windshield.

OTHER CHURCH OCCASIONS

A Christening

A christening is yet another happy occasion made more festive with plenty of flowers. What better first gift could a child have than to be surrounded by loving family and flowers?

As well as a pedestal design – or several if the church is large enough – you could have ceremonial brass candlestands which look lovely when specially dressed for the day.

Use long-lasting flowers, if possible, rather than delicate varieties, and make sure your foam is well soaked because sometimes it is not practical to fix a container to the stand. There is generally a small rim around the candle, presumably to catch the wax; but it is sometimes possible to fit pieces of floral foam to both sides of the candle. It is advisable to seek permission from whoever is in charge before doing this, however.

Nowadays christenings are conducted within the framework of a church service, not as isolated services. This means, of course, that not only the immediate family but everyone else can enjoy the extra special flower decorations.

Do try to check them a day or so afterwards; nothing looks worse than special arrangements that are fading. No doubt the pedestals and vase designs will last, but try to ensure that everything else is cleaned up and tidied away as soon as it is past its best.

ABOVE White longiflorum lilies, white spray single chrysanthemums and some shapely sprays of white broom dress the Christening candle. Add a white ribbon for this very special occasion.

To decorate a cradle (available from the florist in a choice of pink, blue or white). 1 Fix a flat disc of soaked floral foam to a prong set in the cradle (LEFT). A second round of foam will be needed to achieve the right height, which should be impaled on the first one with the fine cane. 2 Define the basic shape with white ixia and cream altsroemeria (BELOW LEFT). Insert the stems laterally. 3 Add five stems of freesia and a pink ribbon to finish (FAR LEFT)

Church Festivals

ABOVE *Plastic leaves collected over a period of time are the main ingredients of this Christmas design. It has the advantage of being able to be made up in advance – very useful during the busy holiday season. You could add baubles or bells if desired.*

Materials: bronze cherub, ribbon loops. Various gold-plated leaves, handmade poinsettias, gold-painted fir cones.

1 Insert the three long, spiky leaves and use the finest shapes on the outside to give the outline. 2 Put in more leaves, concentrating the heaviest toward the centre, and add the gold-painted fir cones. 3 Place the tallest and smallest poinsettias at the top, and bring the large one to the centre as a focal point. 4 Add red ribbon loops to carry the colour through the design.

It is quite a responsibility as well as a pleasure to arrange flowers for a particular church festival: Easter, Harvest Festival, Christmas or a wedding.

After the weeks of Lent with no flowers at all, the church can be decorated for Easter as lavishly as time, material and money will permit. Daffodils are usually in abundance, together with the new foliage. Many couples who marry at Easter have an extra lovely setting for their wedding.

Lilies are the traditional Easter flower and some churches prefer arums. These certainly are beautiful but are not easy to arrange because of their broad stems. Fortunately, though, they are entirely tolerant of being arranged in foam, provided it is possible to add more water to the container every alternate day or so.

The longiflorum and regale varieties have thinner, more woody stems and are much easier to arrange. They last just as well and also tolerate being arranged in foam provided the water level can be checked from time to time. These lilies are usually transported when they are very young,

ABOVE *This design could have chocolate eggs or an Easter bunny as alternative accessories.*

Materials: tin can with soaked floral foam, cane base, coloured packing straw, two chicks, eggs, Easter ribbon. Freesias, nephrolepsis fern, carnations, spray carnations.

1 Use the freesias and fern for the outline. 2 Add the buds of the spray carnations to the top, and those more open to the centre. Add large carnations to the centre. 3 Add freesias, carnation spray and fern to fill in, bringing them well over the edge of the container. 4 Place the arrangement on the base. 5 Arrange the packing straw on the base with the chicks and eggs. Put the Easter ribbon around the outside of the base.

Special Presentations

SPECIAL FLOWER ARRANGEMENTS

*B*ouquets wrapped in clear cellophane with bright, richly looped bows suggest glamour, success, honour and royal occasions. To add a touch of glamour to a bouquet of flowers from your own garden or from the florist is not difficult and is worth the effort.

You will need cellophane paper, a generous length of water-resistant ribbon and a staple gun. If you can plan ahead, it is well worth having an idea of the colour combination you want in your bouquet before you choose the ribbon, and you can either match one of your colours or perhaps pick a ribbon that makes a strong contrast. Follow the instructions (right) and you will be able to add a touch of luxury to a gift of flowers.

To wrap a gift bouquet, *first make sure that all stems of both flowers and foliage are clean and free from thorns or leaves. 1 Then arrange the flowers and foliage as attractively as possible, longer stems to the back, keeping the shorter ones to the front. Try not to cut stems any shorter than absolutely necessary. 2 Tie the bouquet together at a comfortable tying point with a multi-loop bow of water-resistant ribbon, which has been tied across the centre with a fairly long piece of the same ribbon. It is a good idea to prepare the ribbon at the start. The bouquet should then be laid on the cellophane leaving enough paper to wrap the stems at the bottom and to fold over the flower heads.*

RIGHT The diagram shows the bouquet tied with ribbon and lying on cellophane paper. The arrows indicate how the paper should be folded over the stems and flower heads and tucked underneath the bow. The curved black arrows show how the ties should be first crossed at the back before the final bow is made at the front.

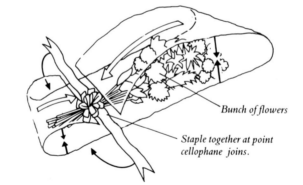

Bunch of flowers

Staple together at point cellophane joins.

1

2

3

4

3 Arrange the cellophane over the flowers and stems so that the ends meet at the tying point. (About twice the length is enough.) 4 Then staple once each side at the tying point, keeping the cross ties outside the paper. 5 Cross the ties at the back and bring around to the front, finishing off with another bow across the centre of the first bow. Staple the edges at least twice, but to prevent the inside from steaming up, be careful not to overseal.

5

The finished gift bouquet of mixed garden flowers wrapped in cellophane paper and tied with a bright, contrasting bow.

Basket Arrangements

For many types of flowers, a basket would seem to be the natural container to choose. They are traditional containers and have for centuries been used all over the world, indeed, all things domestic. Now they are designed specifically for flowers, and are available in a vast range of shapes and sizes from huge curved display baskets to shallow 'Nell Gwyn' shapes, all woven in beautiful natural colours. Wicker and cane can of course be spray-painted to match or complement the arranged flowers and the ribbon for the handle and bows.

They provide endless possibilities for decoration. The materials used to make baskets seem to look right almost anywhere as there is no really strong colour to conflict with existing interior decor. In addition to large arrangements for wedding parties, smaller arrangements can be carried by bridesmaids. They are also suitable for presentation to a visiting dignitary, for example, or for sending to a sick friend in hospital, where the flowers, if properly conditioned, will remain fresh for several days.

To prepare a basket. 1 Choose a ribbon that will harmonize with your proposed design and cut a generous length for binding the basket's handle (about 2-3 times the length will be sufficient).

2 Attach the ribbon securely to the base of the handle with adhesive tape and begin binding.

3 To ensure that the binding does not slip after completion, keep the ribbon pulled taut as you wind. When the handle is covered, secure the end with adhesive tape.

4 With a length of the same coloured ribbon, make a multi-looped bow, keeping the ends long for tying on to the basket.

5 Bind the ends of the ribbon round the centre of the bow and basket handle and tie firmly.

6 Now attach a prong to the inner plastic container with Oasis-fix and place two generous pieces of Oasis-fix on the base of the container.

7 Attach the container to the basket. The whole base will be much firmer if you can now leave it to harden for at least a few hours before beginning your design.

8 Impale a soaked foam block on the prongs; this may be sufficient to hold your design but if the flowers are heavy or the basket is to be transported, secure firmly with more layers of adhesive tape.

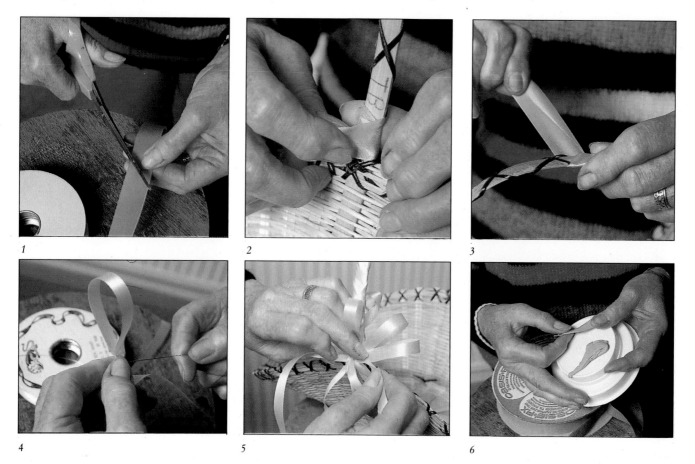

1

2

3

4

5

6

7

8

9

10

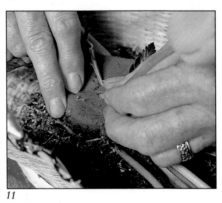
11

12

9 Surround the base with a bed of moss, neatly masking the base sides.

10 Next, take the flowers, remembering to cut the stems to a very sharp point so that they drive crisply into the foam.

11 Begin by inserting yellow tulips, which have been chosen as line flowers. Place tulip buds low down on the basket, placing the well-opened flowers in the middle of the arrangement.

12 The insertion of the tulips is now completed. Add some foliage, including both tulip and daffodil leaves, between the flowers as a background for the next selection of flowers (continued overleaf).

LEFT A shallow basket filled with flowers of a variety of colours. The contrasting wicker handle is interesting enough without the addition of ribbon and would, in any case, prove difficult to bind neatly.

13

14

13 Insert ten daffodils to echo the main lines and establish the height of the arrangement.

14 Position the daffodils so that the angle of each head forms a series of flowing lines around the basket edge.

15 Add small groups of gypsophila stems to fill the spaces between the flowers.

16 The completed basket (BELOW LEFT) to which red alstroemeria has been added to give colour and character to the design.

15

16

RIGHT *The old-fashioned basket was the inspiration for this design. The Edwardians loved ferns, carnations and gypsophila. This arrangement is based on a picture in an old flower book. If you should want to make it look more like a period design, add some fine buttonhole fern, and trail a piece around the handle. Put a large bow of matching ribbon low down on the bare side of the handle.*

Materials: *basket, tin can with soaked floral foam. Spray carnations, gypsophila (baby's breath), ferns, carnations.*

1 Start with the spray carnations at the top and make a diagonal line, leaving a good portion of the handle free. 2 Add gypsophila and ferns, continuing the line. 3 Add the heavier carnations running through the centre of the design, adding more of the spray carnations, gypsophila and ferns as you go to fill the gap.

LEFT *The handle is kept clear so that it can be seen to be a basket, and makes the arrangement easy to carry.*

Materials: *basket with handle, tin can with soaked floral foam. Spanish broom, tulips, pansies, wallflowers (Cheiranthus species, or gillyflower), saxifrage, forget-me-nots.*

1 Place the tin can in the middle of the basket, and make a low outline with the broom. 2 Add the tulips on the outside and bring them to the middle under the handle. 3 Insert the pansies, letting some flow over the side. 4 Add the wallflowers, saxifrage and forget-me-nots to fill in the gaps.

To make a table centrepiece. *1 Mark five lateral points with lily-of-the-valley foliage and mask the foam with molucella and hellebore leaves.*

2 Having marked the tallest point with one stem of spray chrysanthemums, cut five stems of the same type of chrysanthemum to one length and 15 of the spidery variety.

3 Form the outer edge of the design with five of the spidery blooms and place the rest towards the centre to take colour and texture inwards.

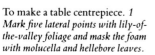

Table Decorations

Table decorations can range from really simple styles, with just a few flowers picked from the garden and put in water, to full-coloured elaborately shaped confections.

The Victorians greatly favoured the epergne. These branched edifices, often made from silver and crystal, were used to grace their dinner tables. They were lavishly decorated with fruit and flowers, usually from the family's hothouses. Very large tables would have several of these confections, and since the material was not concentrated in one place, it would not inhibit lively, across-the-table conversation. This is one of the main points to bear in mind when making your table decoration. It should not be so big as to block the view nor should it be out of scale with the setting.

Wedding Anniversary Arrangements

Flowers make welcome gifts for wedding anniversaries and it is worth taking trouble with decorative centrepieces for anniversary parties.

For this Golden Wedding arrangement, you will need to buy candles and several yards of net. Be generous with the net so that the pleating on each layer can be deep and the finished effect full. You will also need three circles of soaked foam of different sizes, and these should, if possible, be foam and polystyrene posy pads, which can be cut to the diameter you require. Gold spray will be needed to spray the candles, net and foam. The base is made from ½in (15mm) thick wood or cardboard, covered with gold paper.

The all-round point method is used for inserting the flowers, with seven points for the first layer, five for the second and three for the top.

LEFT. This design can be made without the candle; just replace the candle and holder with a flower in the centre, keeping it low in the design.
Materials: covered tin can with soaked floral foam candle holder, candle, cake stand. Michaelmas daisies, chrysanthemums, Alchemilla mollis.
1 Place the candle holder in the middle of the floral foam. 2 Insert the cut stems of the Michaelmas daisies to form a low outline. 3 Add chrysanthemums with buds on the outside, the heavier flowers toward the centre. 4 Add more Michaelmas daisies, cutting them short and inserting them between the chrysanthemums. 5 Fill in the gaps with Alchemilla mollis. 6 Place on the cake stand and insert the candle into the holder.*

4 Insert mixed foliage and flowers in the first layer, using the all-round point method. Remember that all the material in the first stage is set in laterally.

5 Insert flowers and foliage into second layer, keeping the stems shorter to maintain the cone effect. Fix them firmly in place.

Golden Wedding Anniversary arrangement. 1 If you cannot buy gold candles, any colour can be sprayed with gold paint. Remember to spray well away from the flowers.

2 The candles should be fitted with wire 'legs' and inserted in the top layer of foam. Pin a strip of gold paper or ribbon around the foam.

3 Pin pleated net to each layer of foam, attaching it to the covered base, and then spray with gold paint.

6 Do the same with the third layer, inserting the candles and finishing off the top with more flowers arranged to form the point of the cone.

LEFT Completed design for a Golden Wedding party.

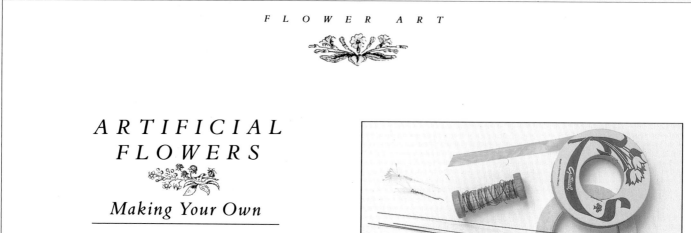

A R T I F I C I A L
F L O W E R S

Making Your Own

Paper flowers can be made by those who enjoy working with crafts, and fake ones made with foil and fabrics are useful for party arrangements.

One paper flower that is very useful is the carnation, which has to be the easiest paper flower of all to make. Buy a roll of crêpe paper, cut off 2in (5cm) from the bottom of the roll and fringe one end. Hold an end of the crepe paper in your left hand with the fringe at the top, and gather the paper with your right hand while turning it with your left. When large enough, wire about ½in (1.3cm) at the base very tightly, then cover the stem with gutta-percha. This can then be used to make attractive Christmas table arrangements, or to blend with holly, ivy and pine. If you are asked to make the arrangements for a club party, such displays cut your cost considerably.

Fabric Flowers

Some people dislike the very thought of using imitation or permanent flowers and, certainly, there can be no substitute for the real thing, which is constantly changing, seasonal, exciting and sometimes unpredictable. Yet these flowers and plants that are made to imitate nature so exactly have a place in today's life-styles. They demand no conditioning, they will stay in place as they have been arranged and they will not wilt from lack of water.

Daffodils, daisies, ferns, gladioli, poppies and roses are all meticulously reproduced in a variety of sizes, colour, shapes and textures. In fact, there are very few flowers that are not now reproduced. There are also flowering plants, such as petunias, geraniums, hydrangeas and agapanthus, wisteria and laburnum, plus many other plants which are correct in every detail and so convincing in appearance that one almost feels the need to water them.

Silk flowers are beautiful in their own right, and have the added bonus of being washable and if swished gently round in warm soapy water, rinsed and hung up to dry. They are reasonably priced, and of course can be used over and over again. They are also useful for party arrangements: if one gets bumped against or knocked over, it won't come to much harm. Also, the busy hostess can make up such an arrangement days in advance.

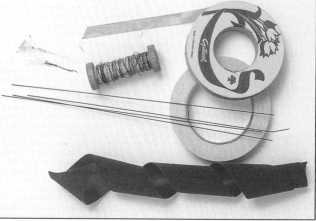

1

2

3

To make a poinsettia: *you will need: red flocked non-fraying ribbon; adhesive tape; real flower stamens; fine reel wire and sturdier wire; green crêpe paper or gutta-percha.*

1 Cut five, long, tapering petals from the red ribbon. 2 Using lengths of sturdy wire, tape one to back of each petal using red adhesive tape. 3 Turn petals face upward. 4 Using fine reel wire, attach stamens to one petal. 5 Add second petal, wiring it to first. 6 Bind in remaining petals, one by one. 7 Cover stem with gutta-percha or thin strips of crêpe paper. 8 Bend petals out and curve ends over slightly.

4

5

6

7

8

There are a few facts you should take into consideration when using artificial flowers to their full advantage:

When buying permanent flowers and foliage, try to buy the best possible quality. These will withstand wind and weather, and having near permanent colours, will not fade in bright sunlight.

Use flowers that would normally be in season – don't use silk daffodils in high summer, or chrysanthemums in spring.

Although the arrangements will last, don't keep them for more than two weeks – after that no one will notice them. Either take them out of the container and rearrange them in a different container and design, or store them in a box and make up a new arrangement with different flowers.

Permanent flowers should be arranged with as much care as one gives to living material and the foam should be properly masked with either moss or foliage. In my view, bows of ribbon inserted into the centre of an arrangement do not make a substitute for careful masking. By all means add one or two bows if they enhance the general appearance of the arrangement. Be prepared to remove any unsightly stems and replace them with wire and tape.

'Cheating' is allowed: use artificial flowers with fresh foliage – they look unbelievably realistic this way.

Make a few curves in some of the wire stems to avoid a stiff look; this will make the arrangement look more natural.

One method that gives more control over the flowers – it can be used for artificial foliage too – is to remove the side shoots from flowers, such as a spray of roses, and give them a false stem with stub wire. Fold the stub wire not quite in half, lay the shorter piece of wire about 1½in (3.8cm) along the stem, and wind the longer piece around the stem and wire three or four times, pulling the wire firm. Then place both pieces of wire alongside each other, and cover all the wire with gutta-percha, a kind of masking tape.

This method lets you place your materials in your design much more easily. It creates a natural effect, too, for you are using the artificial material in the same way that you would use fresh plant material.

Fabric flower and foliage arrangements should be based in Oasis-sec or a similar product: ordinary foam used dry is not nearly firm enough and may easily break apart. Drihard is another product that gives an extremely firm base, but being a type of cement it dries not only very hard but very fast. Thus one needs to work with both speed and precision since there is rarely a chance to change your mind once a stem has been placed.

Both foam base and Drihard should be masked, either with grey reindeer moss or ordinary green moss, both of which should be soaked in clean water to make them supple. The moss can then be pinned to the base with small wire hairpins: it quickly dries, retaining its original colour.

2

3

4

1

To make a fabric flower arrangement. *1 Collect fabric flowers and foliage together in groups before preparing a container. Bright, mixed-coloured flowers have been chosen for this display.*

2 First cut the correct size of brown floral foam and wedge it into the neck of a container and mask it with green moss.

3 Arrange the moss carefully so that moss and fabric foliage will appear very natural together.

4 Set the vertical and main lateral lines in position. The lateral material is set well back in the foam block to leave the front free.

RIGHT *A spring design of daffodils, freesias and polyanthus in a dove-grey compote.*

Choose whichever moss blends better with the flowers: for example, spring flowers, daffodils, freesias and poly-anthus would look more realistic based with green moss, while most dried material and the pale browns and creams of some fabric flowers look better with the reindeer moss.

Ornamental 'Flowers'

Some fabric flowers are purely decorative and do not faithfully resemble any living material: they are useful simply from the point of view of colour, shape and size. Then there are those that are blatantly imitation, but that are still very decorative and fun to use. For example, huge gold and silver open roses, which, if used in the right place at the right time, are really effective. They can be used for gold or silver anniversaries, at Christmas or birthday parties, or to decorate a special gift-wrapped parcel.

This brings us on to the now outmoded plastic flowers, frowned upon by many. Yet even these may in certain circumstances have a decorative value – you could, for instance, try spraying them with gold or silver and using them in Christmas arrangements. Strangely enough, you can buy plastic Christmas roses, and because their texture is so similar to the real thing these look quite attractive used with fresh greenery. You can also put some of them on false stems, as they come with a stem length of only 6in (15cm), and some longer stems will give a wide variety of designs. With white waxy candles you can make a pretty design to use at Christmas.

PRESSED FLOWER PRESENTATIONS

BELOW *A leaf calendar, the design for which was assembled quickly and confidently by an assured young artist.*

The traditional setting for a pressed flower design always used to be a picture frame. Pictures are still, of course, one of the most effective and versatile methods of presentation, and there is always room for imaginative improvisation, especially when working with children. We are fortunate today, however, in being able to buy an enormous variety of attractive settings specifically designed for craft work. And even this most traditional of crafts is now being influenced by the introduction of modern techniques and materials.

Children's Presentations

Making designs from flowers and leaves which they have pressed themselves can be a satisfying and pleasurable activity for children. It may not always be easy, however, for teachers to find suitable methods of presentation, attractive, and yet, at the same time, inexpensive and simple enough for the children to handle without too much adult help.

When working with young children, the 'rule' that pressed flower designs must always be protected is abandoned. Unprotected designs may not last very long, but they give real pleasure during the making. And with the right sort of flowers and 'settings', they should survive the perilous journey home, and last quite long enough to give pleasure to families and friends.

It is a good idea to suggest to the children that they lay out their whole design on their chosen background before sticking anything down. The sticking stage is an important one for unprotected designs. Children should be advised that too much glue will spoil their work, but too little could also put it at risk. It is therefore necessary to use more than the single spot recommended for protected work. Several tiny spots should be applied to the back of each item, which should then be carefully and firmly smoothed down.

Children's Calendars

Acquire some pieces of sturdy card, preferably in varying colours, and cut them to a variety of different sizes. (Try asking the local printer or art shop for offcuts.) Ask the children to spread out their pressed material, and to select a background suitable for the design they intend. If they are

capable of line work, suggest that they use a coloured felt-tip pen and ruler to outline their design area, as on the heather calendar. Once the design is complete, it is a simple matter to attach a calendar booklet and a 'hanger' made from a loop of ribbon, with some good adhesive tape.

Children's Bookmarks

These can be made of thin card, cut to a suitable shape. If you have a means of cutting an attractive deckled edge, or if your artists are able to outline the card, so much the better, but neither of these processes is essential. The role of bookmark should be a perfect one for a pressed flower design: for if it is used for its intended purpose, it remains pressed flat within a protective book. Nevertheless, it is important to stick the flowers down carefully, and to emphasize that the finished product is delicate, and needs careful handling.

BELOW A simple, sturdy heather calendar. The design is outlined in blue felt tip pen.

BELOW Ribbon bookmarks protected with a manageably small area of covering film.

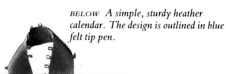

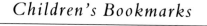

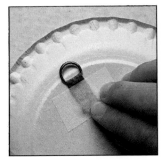

ABOVE *Prepare a paper plate picture for hanging by attaching a small curtain ring to its back with a short length of ribbon and some adhesive tape.*

LEFT *Paper plate pictures made from flowers which are sturdy enough to remain unprotected: buttercups, daisies, larkspur and anaphalis.*

Children's Paper Plate Pictures

The paper plate has several advantages as a method of presenting pictures. It allows children to work within a circular outline for a change, and the plate rim serves as an attractive frame for the picture and gives it some protection. Moreover, paper plates are now available in a variety of interesting colours. The best means of hanging such a picture is probably to attach a small curtain ring to the back of it by means of a short length of ribbon and some adhesive tape.

Children's Polystyrene Tray Pictures

A good alternative to the paper plate is the sort of flat container used by many supermarkets for packaging meat. If you can collect enough (well washed!) trays like this, they make attractive settings for flower work. Children may find it difficult to work within their fairly deep recesses. If this is the case, make the task easier – and the finished effect more interesting – by cutting a piece of sturdy coloured paper to the size of the inside of the base. The design should be stuck on to this paper, which can then be carefully glued into the tray. A bonus point for this type of setting is that it can quite easily be covered with 'cling film' (plastic wrap). This ensures a longer, more dust-free life. Use a curtain ring 'hanger' as on the paper plate.

Greetings Cards

These can be made in much the same way as the bookmarks described above. They should be folded in half before beginning design work. You may choose to reflect the main design with a smaller one inside the card.

Unusual Presentations for Adults: Varnishing

Ordinary household varnish is a good means of protection, provided that a suitable background is selected and the right pressed material used. The range of possible flowers for this work is somewhat limited because they must be neither too thick for the varnish to seal them effectively nor so fine that they 'disappear' into their protective coating. Most of the flowers previously recommended for unprotected work can be used with this technique. The illustrations in this section show that love-in-a-mist (devil-in-a-bush) and lobelia are also good subjects.

The background should be smooth and not too absorbent – stone, wood, cork and wax are all possibilities (see below). The technique for applying varnish and flowers is the same in each case: prepare the surface of the background, making sure it is smooth, clean and dust-free; plan the design by placing the flowers on to the background in the positions they will eventually take up, transfer this design to a temporary surface while applying the first thin coat of varnish; then, while the varnish is still wet, position the flowers in it. (There is, of course, no need to use any glue – a great advantage of this procedure is that, for the first 15 minutes or so, it is possible to use a cocktail stick to move the flowers around in the fluid varnish, until they are perfectly positioned.) The design should then be allowed to dry for at least eight hours in a dust-free place, before the second protective coat is applied.

Pebble Paperweights

The first requirement is of course to find some suitable stones. The large, smooth, flattish seashore pebbles are ideal – look for those with the most interesting shapes and colours. It is a good idea to examine them while they are still wet, for although a beautiful glistening pebble often dries to a more nondescript appearance, the subtle colour variations will re-appear when the varnish is applied.

Wall Plaques: Cork

Cork makes an attractive and interesting background, and is easily obtainable in the form of square wall tiles or round table-mats. Use bright flowers so that they stand out against the strong colour of the cork. Hang by the curtain-ring and ribbon method.

Wall Plaques: Wood

Woods have so many different colours and grain patterns that it should be easy to find suitable pieces. The simplest and cheapest way of acquiring these is to buy offcuts of plywood. The appropriate size and shape depend very much on the nature of the intended design; make sure that the surface and edges are smooth. In the examples shown here, the plywood is so thin that it can be cut to attractive shapes with scissors. Lightweight plaques can be made to hang in the same way as paper plate pictures, whereas the heavier ones need hooks attached with screws.

ABOVE These wall plaques have been cut from the thinnest possible plywood. They were scorched around the edge to make an attractive outline before designs made with montbretia, heather and fuchsia were varnished on.

BELOW Pebble paperweights. Simple designs of lobelia and larkspur have been varnished on to these pebbles.

BELOW Cork-mat wall plaques with a varnished design of buttercups and cow parsley.

POT POURRI

Pot pourri were originally used to help counteract unpleasant smells and ward off diseases. Today they are just as useful for making any room in the house smell pleasant and welcoming.

There are two types of pot pourri – dry and moist. They are very easy to make and can be kept in open dishes but their perfume will last longer if they are kept in closed jars or pots and the lid removed occasionally, when the room is in use, to let the scent escape.

Refresher pot pourri oils are available for reviving the scent of pot pourri; a few drops of an essential oil on a dry mixture and oil, brandy, or eau-de-cologne on a moist one.

There are many different mixtures, recipes and variations of recipes for pot pourri, but all contain ingredients belonging to the same four basic categories: one or more main perfuming ingredient, some background perfumes, a fixative, and a preservative.

Of the main perfuming ingredients, sweet-scented rose petals and lavender are very popular traditional perfuming ingredients but any other strongly scented dried flowers can be used, such as carnation, lilac, jasmine, honeysuckle, lily-of-the-valley, magnolia, hyacinth, orange blossom and mock orange blossom, peony, lime flower and chamomile.

Smaller amounts of other scented ingredients are added to give depth to the perfume. Such ingredients include scented leaves like the sweet geraniums, bay, lemon balm and marjoram, spices and dried fruit peels.

Cinnamon, cloves, allspice, nutmeg, mace, coriander and cardamom are the most frequently used spices. Whole spices should be freshly coarsely ground or crushed in a pestle and mortar as ready-ground spices soon lose their aroma and will stick to the sides of glass containers. Occasionally, whole cloves, whole coriander seeds, pieces of mace and small pieces of cinnamon stick are added for appearance's sake.

Essential oils, available from chemists and herbalists must be added drop by drop and the ingredients stirred after the addition of each drop as they are very powerful and will spoil the balance of the perfumes if added in too-large amounts. It is better to use a combination of oils than a larger amount of one type if making large amounts of pot pourri.

A fixative is an ingredient that is added to marry all the different fragrances together and slow down the evaporation of the fragrant essential oils. Violet-scented powdered dried orris root appears most often as a fixative with powdered resin of gum benzoin being the second most popular choice. The essential oil of sandalwood or sandalwood powder can also be used.

Thinly pare the rind from an orange or lemon then rub the rind with orris root, place on a wire rack and dry in a very cool oven until crisp.

An ingredient that will prevent the pot pourri mixture from decaying is also necessary. Bay salt used to be used but nowadays a non-iodised salt, such as sea salt, is normally incorporated. Dry it in a low oven for several hours before using it.

A small cotton or muslin sachet of silica gel buried in a pot pourri mixture will help to keep it dry.

SWEET-SCENTED POT POURRI

DRY

100g/1oz dried scented rose petals

·

25g/100oz dried lily-of-the-valley

·

25g/1oz dried clove pinks

·

25g/1oz dried sweet peas

·

15g/½oz dried rosemary

·

15g/½oz dried thyme

·

2 tablespoons crushed dried lemon rind

·

2 tablespoons crushed dried orange rind

·

1 tablespoon bruised cloves

·

4 tablespoons powdered orris root

·

5 drops oil of bergamot

·

Gum benzoin

Mix the first nine ingredients together and leave for 2 days. Stir in the gum benzoin and orris root then the oil of bergamot, drop by drop. Cover tightly and leave for 6 weeks, stirring occasionally. Transfer to china or glass bowls.

SWEET-SANDALWOOD POT POURRI

MOIST

2 parts dried rose petals

•

1 part dried peonies

•

1 part dried orange blossom

•

salt (see above)

•

fixative and spice mixture
(to 4½/1 gallon caked petals)

•

15g/½oz powdered sandalwood

•

2 tablespoons dried lemon thyme

•

1 tablespoon dried bergamot

•

1 tablespoon dried rosemary

•

1 tablespoon crumbled bay leaves

•

crushed dried rind of 1 orange

•

15g/½oz freshly ground cinnamon

•

15g/½oz freshly ground cloves

•

15g/½oz freshly ground allspice

•

40g/1½oz orris root powder

Mix the dried flowers together, measure their volume then measure out an appropriate amount of salt. Layer the flowers and salt in a deep, wide-necked earthenware pot, until the pot is full. Cover tightly and leave in a dark but airy place for at least two weeks, longer if possible. If you do not have enough petals to fill the pot at first, more can be added over several days. Stir the contents well before adding more layers.

The flowers and salt should form a solid, dry cake. Tip this out and break it up. Stir in the fixative and spice mixture using a wooden spoon, blending the ingredients together well. Put back into the pot, cover tightly to seal and leave for 5–6 weeks, shaking or stirring frequently. Transfer to small pottery jars.

Index

Acknowledgements

Royal Horticultural Society:
16(l), 17(t)
Scala, Florence: 9(b)
Edwin Smith: 18(b)
Sotheby's, London: 15
Trustees of British Museum: 8(r)
Visual Arts Library, London: 14(t)
Yale Center for British Art, New Haven: 13(c)

l = left, r = right, b = bottom, t = top, c = centre
Artothek, Munich: 16(r)
Bodleian Library: 12(l), 13(r)
British Library, London: 11
E. T. Archive: 14(l)
Vana Haggerty: 8(l), 9(t), 17(bl&r), 18(t)
Musée des Beaux Arts, Lille: 12(r)